CRUISING

THE PACIFIC COAST

Mexico to Alaska

Second Edition

Cruising

The Pacific Coast

Mexico to Alaska

Carolyn & Jack
WEST

Miller Freeman Publications, Inc.
500 Howard Street
San Francisco, California
1970

Miller Freeman Publications, Inc.
San Francisco, California

Library of Congress Catalog Card No. 76-121230

Printed in the United States of America

Contents

List of Charts

PHOTO CREDITS, other than authors':

Army Corps of Engineers, Portland, Oregon; Diana Beeston; British Columbia Government, Department of Recreation & Conservation; Bryant's Marina, Inc.; California State Parks & Recreation Department; Val Hennell; Ray Krantz; Los Angeles County; Harry Merrick; Frank Morris; Jan Mower; Noyo Harbor District; Oregon State Highway Department; Bob O'Neil; Port of Coos Bay, Oregon; Port of Los Angeles, Calif.; Port of San Diego, Calif.; Port of Seattle, Wash.; Santa Barbara News Press; Lola Thompson; Union Pacific Railroad; United States Coast Guard; Washington State Parks & Recreation Commission; Dick Whittington.

Introduction

The pages of this book were completely blank twenty-five years ago, at the time when we desperately needed the help and guidance of others who had cruised the Pacific Coast. True, the *Coast Pilot* books were available then, but they were written mainly for merchant seamen and their deep-draft, ocean-going vessels manned by professional crews.

We were then commissioning the first of our long-range power boats, in Seattle, where we had acquired from the Maritime Commission one of the surplus 104-foot rescue craft. We were literally up to our Plimsoll line in problems—repowering the ship with diesel engines, removing tons of military gear which had served its war purpose, replacing specialized electronic navigation equipment with units that we understood and could use, and trying to find an amateur crew from among our friends to help us bring the ship down the coast to her home port in San Pedro, California.

The day finally came when we departed from Puget Sound for the southbound trip, armed with every available chart and government publication, including lists of world-wide radio aids, although we were only interested in this one segment of the world. But still we had nothing as a reference or guide to small harbors that we might use for refuge, or any reports which would help us on our first long-distance trip. It was, nevertheless, a successful passage, non-stop from Seattle to San Pedro.

We vowed then that someday we would compile a cruising guide to Pacific Coast waters that would give cruising-boat owners some of the more intimate details of harbors, weather conditions, and facilities available—hence this book.

Within these pages are our findings based on more than 125,000 miles of cruising the Pacific Coast, aboard the first *Monsoon* or our second ship, the 72-foot *Monsoon II,* and aboard

1

friends' cruisers. The first *Monsoon* logged a distance of nearly twice around the world, and *Monsoon II* has logged somewhat more. All of this has been without professional crews with ourselves as the Commodore and Captain of our ships, and without any major incidents of danger or hazard.

Over the years we have written many thousands of words, in article form, for national boating journals. Each time, however, much had to be omitted in the interest of confining a many-months' trip to a few pages of magazine size. Invariably there would be letters asking for more information on weather, harbors, supplies available, and cruising conditions, indicating a growing interest in the area.

Any cruising area spanning a distance of nearly four thousand miles can be expected to have wide contrasts in climates, scenery and cruising conditions. Few realize, however, that the Pacific Coast has, in addition, wide contrasts in the nationality of its discoverers. Among them are the Spanish, whose influence predominates in the names given bays and capes from Cape San Lucas to Cape Mendacino; the native American Indians, whose stockades, forts and villages are still important landmarks along the Oregon coastline, northward into British Columbia and Alaska; again the Spanish, who discovered the Strait of Juan de Fuca separating Canada and the State of Washington; the English, who charted and named such islands as Vancouver, Whidbey and Bainbridge in Puget Sound and British Columbian waters, and finally the Russians and Scandinavians who first settled Alaska.

So international is the background of Pacific Coast cruising waters that it took Kaiser Wilhelm of Germany to act as arbitrator between the British and Americans to stop a near war between the two countries. The dispute arose over the location of the international boundary, which the English claimed should be through Rosario Strait, to the east of the San Juan Islands, while the United States claimed it should be through Haro Strait, west of the 172-island archipelago. Fortunately the near war was settled by Wilhelm and the boundary established through Haro Strait about 1890, when the present State of Washington was a part of the Oregon Territory.

Geographically there is little similarity between East and West coasts, even on identical lines of latitude. On the western shorelines of Mexico, California, Oregon and Washington, nature has given us few natural harbors, clusters of protective islands or miles of inland waterways. The half-century lead in the development of East Coast waterways and harbors will never be equaled on the West Coast, due to the very nature of the coastline—notwithstanding the scores of man-made harbors that have recently been built or are scheduled for development.

Conversely, the Pacific shores have some startling advantages for the off-shore sailor: uniformly deep waters, insect-free climates, absence of hurricane weather; the warm flow of the Japanese current, which keeps harbors ice-free the year around as far north as Juneau, Alaska; and many delightful harbors, unspoiled by tourism and its attending noise and confusion.

Those with sincere love of the sea and of the life it affords when afloat will find destinations on the Pacific Coast totally foreign to their city-side home life. Their boats offer them a complete respite, change and challenge while plying the Pacific's contrasting shores. But the skipper must, for the most part, take his own boat. Few charter boats are available here for long-range cruising; and again in contrast with the Atlantic seaboard, there is a dearth of fancy shoreside facilities except in the few large ports.

To those who have read some of the few published reports of specific pleasure cruises along Pacific waters and into the Gulf of Baja California—and in so doing have decided "that's too rigorous, too hard-chancing for me!"—let's first consider these factors: 1) Did the author choose the most favorable time of year for his sail or cruise? 2) Was he a seasoned navigator on a well-founded vessel, and was the boat of a proper type for the waters he plied? 3) Did he visit a foreign country with prejudices stacked high on his shoulders? 4) Did he overcrowd his boat with guests who were unacquainted with the sea?

The fable of the three blind men feeling diverse parts of an elephant and being asked to describe "what is an elephant like?" is perhaps analogous to a writer who, through ignorance or misinformation, is guilty of portraying an untrue word picture of a visited land or body of water.

It is with the thought of writing informatively and objectively (after having "felt all of the elephant and having seen it visually") that we have prepared this book. We have purposely plotted our course from southeast to the northwest because, with the exception of the Gulf area of Baja California this heading presents the more difficult run from a weather and sea-condition standpoint. Shelter must be taken more often on a northwest run upcoast from prevailing winds and ocean currents. This heading will also take one into many harbors which otherwise he might delete from his itinerary, when sailing or cruising down the coast with weather and seas behind him.

At the end of each of the three Parts of this book is a section covering: fuel, water and supplies; navigational aids; harbor facilities; communications; distances; customs procedures for foreign ports, and other pertinent data.

Whether your boat is power or sail, large or small, with or without a crew—the harbors, the people at them and the grandeur of the Pacific coast will be the same. So join us now, if you will, on this 4000-mile cruise from the upper reaches of the Gulf of Baja California, southeast to the tip of the Cape and northwest up the coast to our ultimate destination of Juneau, Alaska.

PART I

CRUISING BAJA CALIFORNIA

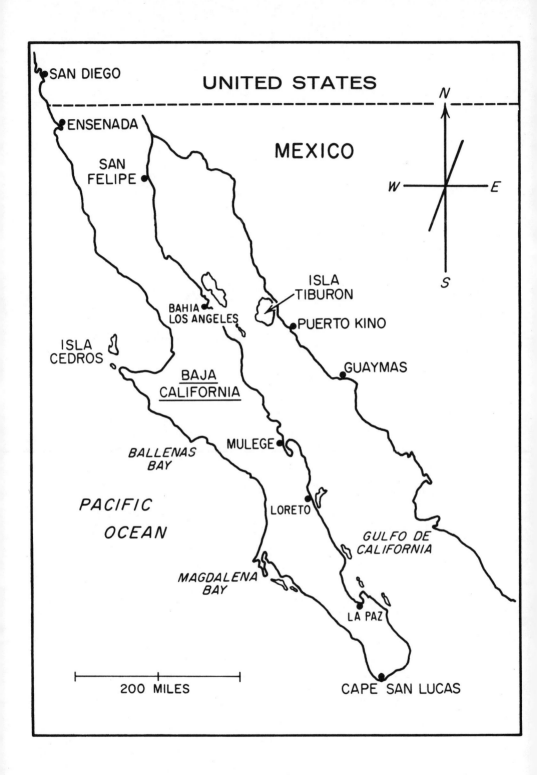

CHAPTER 1

Broad Aspects

The Peninsula of Lower (Baja) California, lying between the 32nd parallel and the Tropic of Cancer off Mexico's western coast, has since its discovery in 1532 stubbornly resisted both industry and extensive colonization. This is principally due to its relative isolation and general lack of fresh water.

From the U.S./Mexican border south some 500 miles, there are several fertile valleys which through rainfall and irrigation are now producing fairly extensive crops. A similar, though smaller subtropical zone at the southern tip of the Peninsula produces excellent fruits and vegetables raised for both local and export trade. But most of this 1,016-mile-long stretch of mountain and desert land, varying from 40 to 200 miles in width, is an arid yet spectacular wilderness. From 10,000-foot, snow-covered mountain peaks to the palm-fringed river of Mulege (Moo-la-hay) on to its sear desert areas of cactus and elephant trees—the Peninsula's topography is ever awesome in contrasts.

Except for the few short spurs of good highways from the border to Ensenada on the Pacific side and to San Felipe on the Gulf side, the word "road," as applied to Baja California, is a euphemism. A few hardy travelers with jeeps, campers or motorcycles have made the long, rough journey from border to the Cape. But these sprawling trail-like roads are so miserable, so ill-defined and torturous to vehicle and human alike, that this mode of Peninsula travel is little used.

With the exception of Guaymas, Puerto Kino and Mazatlan on the Mexican mainland, to which there are good roads for trailed boats, there are no other harbors of any consequence to entice the pleasure cruiser. Topographically this shore is flat, barren and monotonous down to a point approaching Mazatlan. From there on, the coastline changes to another world of tropical greenery.

7

Until the early 1940's, a half-dozen pleasure boats per year were perhaps the total number that cruised from the United States down to the Peninsula's semi-tropical waters. Now over a thousand pleasure boats per year cruise down the ocean coast, and many hundreds more trail their boats overland to such sites as San Felipe or Puertocitos at the head of the Gulf, or to Guaymas and Puerto Kino on the Mexican mainland. Improved highways leading to the Gulf and modern trailer equipment have contributed largely to the influx of small boats to this oft-termed "Sea of Cortez."

There are many highly-varied reasons for seeking vacation along these shores. For those who cruise or sail just for the water-borne interval, or for the boat-handling involved in getting there

Typical Gulf-island anchorage. This is situated at the southwestern end of Angel de la Guarda Island.

(or anywhere) and back, it offers just that. For the ardent fisherman, the Gulf is renowned for its angling rewards. For those seeking sunshine and warm waters during northern latitudes' winter season, this too is an asset in Mexican cruising. The spa-seeker, however, had best look elsewhere. Though improved facilities are upgrading La Paz, Mulege and the Cape San Lucas area, there are still few shoreside attractions to tempt those who seek the ultimate in sophisticated surroundings.

To know something of the inhabitants of Mexico, their temperament, customs and ways of life, is a definite asset in a visit to their land. Their lives are slower-paced than ours, and if this fact is not taken into consideration, nothing but frustration develops. If you plan in advance that every negotiation made in Mexico will take perhaps twice the time it would at home, you will be about right. Don't fret—this cannot be changed. Sit on a curb and study your Spanish dictionary while you wait, or relax with a beer in a cantina. Try to emulate your host's relaxation.

In the smaller Mexican harbor settlements it is customary to take ashore some small gifts, such as candy for the children or perhaps .22 shells or fish-hooks for the men, many of whom depend upon hunting and fishing for a major part of their diet. In larger communities it is also customary upon arrival to engage an agent to handle customs papers and to act as supplies-purchaser, translator, package carrier, procurer of transportation and in short, to be an over-all representative. Arrange the business details first—what you expect of him, for how long and for how many pesos. When in agreement, proceed to enjoy your stay in port.

Before taking your boat from the U.S. across the Mexican border, you will need to arrange with a broker or the Mexican Consulate for clearance papers for delivery to the Port Captain at the first major port of entry in Mexico, where they will be endorsed for continuation. It is also advisable to exchange U.S. currency for Mexican money in the amount you anticipate spending during your stay in Mexico. For some years the rate of exchange has been 12.50 pesos for one American dollar. With few exceptions, only near-bordertown merchants will accept American currency. Traveler's checks are accepted at most of the resort hotels and at banks in larger cities, but cashing a personal check, if possible at all, often involves a delay of up to two weeks' time. Food and staples are for the most part less expensive than in the U.S. Ship's

Sea turtles are brought in at Bahia de Los Angeles.

fuel and engine parts, where obtainable, will cost more than Stateside counterparts due to the Peninsula's basic scarcity of transportation for imports.

Whether or not one plans to fish in Mexican waters, it is advisable to buy a fishing license at the start of a trip. The cost is slight, and because most people cruise south expressly to fish, Mexican officials expect this added revenue. For those intending to hunt, both gun and hunting permits must also be obtained.

Wearing apparel for this area is basically informal. Take what you will for an average temperature of 75 to 85 degrees in the Gulf, and warmer wear for the windy coolness of the ocean side. Although in the past women were expected to wear skirts rather than slacks ashore, this custom is no longer so pronounced. Due to the fact that shore-going often involves precarious steps, ladders, etc., to docks or sometimes damp surf landings in a shore-boat, most women find slacks or culottes more functional than a skirt. Dresses may be either too tight for a wide step or too full for windy weather. With the exception of Ensenada, La Paz and some resort hotels, laundry facilities on the Peninsula are primitive and dry cleaners almost nonexistent. Drip-drys and cottons are therefore favored for easy maintenance.

Proper equipment and supplies for the boat will of course depend on its size, type and proposed itinerary. Specific suggestions in this category, as well as notes on the shoreside facilities that are available at various ports, appear at the end of Part I. In general, it should be emphasized that for small craft with limited fuel and water capacity, gasoline and pure drinking water may be ordered to be sent ahead by native boat to a designated harbor. This is customary procedure for most trailed boats entering the Gulf, as well as for those with limited capacity traveling down the peninsula's Pacific Ocean side. The person to contact regarding boat launching and refueling at any port will change from year to year, so there is little point in specifying any particular person. The possibility of there being several to serve you is far more likely than is the off-chance that you may need to inquire for your needs. A chamois for straining gasoline and a fuel-transfer pump should be included in the trailed boat's equipment, along with an accurate compass, charts, and if at all possible, a depth-sounder and marine radio.

Tidal ranges run high in the upper Gulf, with a fluctuation of 20 to 30 feet at San Felipe Bay, diminishing gradually to about 14 feet at Willard Bay and 6 feet at Puerto Kino. As the Gulf widens to the south, tide ranges return to normal for the latitude. Because of these varied extremes, care must be taken when leaving an anchored boat, even for a short time. There are no pub-

Street scene, San Jose del Cabo.

lished tide tables for the Gulf, but conversions can be made from U.S. Pacific Coast Tables, using San Diego, California, as a point of reference. Such conversions as applied to Gulf waters will of course prove more accurate in the lower and wider reaches than in the upper latitudes, due to the latter's constricting topography.

Although the upper Gulf may be cruised the year around, the summer and fall months are extremely hot and muggy with temperatures averaging well over 100 degrees—fine for fishing, but debilitating to the fisherman. December to June is the best over-all weather for Gulf cruising. At the time of autumnal equinox (September and early October), there are apt to be violent southerlies which blow with little forewarning; it is therefore the one interval to avoid, especially in southern Cape latitudes and along the Peninsula's Pacific shore.

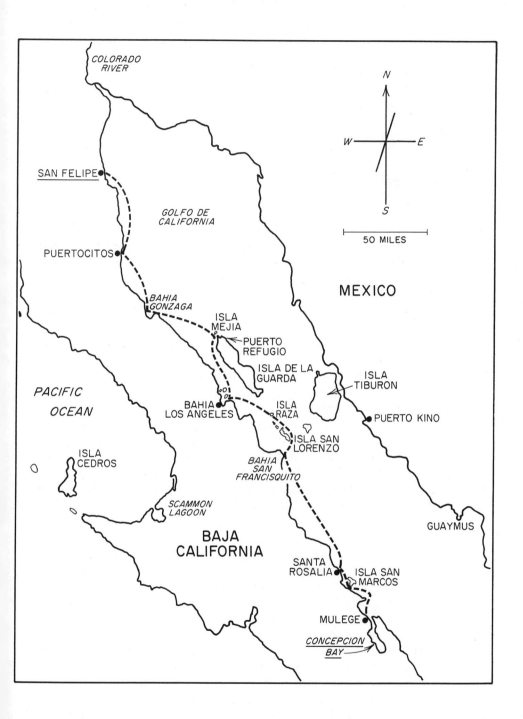

CHAPTER 2

San Felipe to Concepcion Bay

At the far northern end of Baja's Gulf, utter silence first greets the senses. At San Felipe, a trailed boat has just been launched. It bobs soundlessly under a hot morning sun. For a few moments the people aboard are motionless, shading their eyes against the glare. Blue Gulf waters shimmer off to an infinity of hazy purple ramparts. A barren shoreline, shading from gray to tan, sweeps up and away to recede in a distant horizon—the exact pale blue of the sky.

"You wouldn't exactly call this a 'marina' would you?"—the small-boat skipper finally spoke. "I guess this is what is meant by 'getting away from it all.'" Although there were others in the harbor—native fishing boats, several outboards and our own heavy cruiser, there was still the feeling of our being mere props on an improbable, dreamlike stage. From the violet-colored heights of 10,126-foot Calamajue Mountain, Baja's highest peak, down to San Felipe's hot sand shore, the scene appeared one of suspended animation. We felt as if transfixed in some nebulous mirage.

The trailed boat's engine started then, and its abrupt sound shattered the still morning air. But the noise was only momentary. The boat gathered speed and moved swiftly southward, its sound and wake rolling up like a carpet behind it. Soon it was a speck—a gnat on a flat blue plate. San Felipe's little huddle of dusty dwellings closed their shutters and returned to sleep.

This solemn place is the trailed boat's principal access to Baja California's waters, now that a good road joins it with Mexicali on the U.S./Mexican border. Until the road was built it was a vacation area available only to boats capable of the long ocean haul down the peninsula's Pacific ocean side, around the Cape and up the Gulf some 800 miles. This, in fact, had been our route to San Felipe on *Monsoon II*. It was mid-April and we with

At San Felipe, tidal changes range as high as 20 feet. Local fishing boats seldom bother to anchor beyond low-tide mark, but visiting boats should do so.

our guests, Sue and Joe Kelly, had been cruising nearly a month before finally reaching this northern Gulf apex.

"And that fellow told me they just left Los Angeles three days ago." Joe waved an arm in reference to the cruiser now receding in the distance. "He said the first day they were here they caught a 40-pound grouper and two totuavas weighing over 100 pounds apiece!"

We agreed with Joe that the small boat's occupants were lucky on both counts: their quick ingress to the Gulf, compared to our own, and their sizeable fish catch—though the latter was not surprising. Here in this giant fishbowl the waters are continually agitated from above and below, for besides the abundance of game fish the sea teems with surface action. Depending on the season, gray whales, porpoise, huge manta rays and sea lions are ever surfacing and disporting themselves. Gulls, terns and cormorants vie noisily with the silent pelican, each trying to outmaneuver the other for fish or plankton.

In contrast, the bordering shores are quite devoid of life. A few transient native fishermen are in evidence at certain seasons, but for the most part there is little left to indicate how well-populated the peninsula was, as historians * inform us, up to the sixteenth century. Scientists' Carbon-14 tests are now disclosing that this northern region contains some of the largest kitchen middens in the world, testifying to the vast Indian population living here two to six thousand years ago.

This year's trip, our fourth cruise into the Gulf, was purposely started in March. Previously we had cruised the Sea of Cortez in winter months, November to February, but differing opinions as to the weather and sea conditions encountered and whether insects were a problem during warmer weather prompted this later start for a first-hand comparison. For the Kellys, it was strictly a vacation and an introduction to Gulf cruising. They have a 42-foot Angleman ketch which they were planning to take into Mexican waters after sampling the area with us. (This they subsequently did. See "Coasting Down to Acapulco in a Breeze," Nov. '65 *Popular Boating* magazine.) As for ourselves, it was another combination business-and-pleasure cruise to gather more material for our various writing projects.

"Well, we've seen what the upper Gulf is like," we told the Kellys. "Let's haul up the anchor and do some harbor-hopping on our way south."

Sue looked up from the history book she had been reading. "Do you know what Father Jacob Baegert wrote in 1863?" she asked. "He said there was a tribe of about 40,000 Cocopaha Indians living around here then, and that they were all nudists!"

Joe looked at Sue's bikini and laughed: "We're pretty close to that state right now, aren't we?" We were indeed all wearing our most scanty attire, in the near ninety-degree heat which fanned out from the Great Sonora Desert to this north-Gulf location.

Once under way, the slight breeze caused by our motion was welcome. We stretched our autopilot's remote control out through a pilothouse window and the four of us gathered on the

---

* *Historical Outline of Lower California*—Francisco Clavijero, 1862. *Three Years Residence in Upper and Lower California*—E. Gould Buffum, 1850.

foredeck—our favorite station to suntan, relax and yet remain on watch.

South of San Felipe the first harbor of any consequence is Puertocitos, 50 miles down the peninsula's eastern shore. A few fishermen with especially sturdy trucks and trailers launch their boats from this cove, but as the road worsens below San Felipe, Puertocitos is not the most favored launching ramp. Twenty-five miles farther southeast the first small group of Gulf islands comes into view, opposite two good refuge coves of Willard and San Luis Gonzaga Bay.

Gonzaga Bay, protected from the southeast, is the larger and more accessible of the two, but Willard anchorage offers protection from both north and south winds. We noticed several small boats at anchor ½ mile or so from the beach in Willard Bay. From their campfire came the tantalizing odors of roasting seafood and wood smoke, and sounds of singing and guitars. Such is the contentment available for cruisers here during periods of calm weather. A few months earlier in the season, we were told, there had been many days of northerly winds, famous for their ability to chop the sea to a froth and to play disquieting tunes through boat rigging.

This is not an area for night running for boats without radar. There are no navigational lights at all and some of the islets near the shoreline are scarcely awash at full tide. By day, however, the islands surrounding these headlands and coves offer an interesting exploration from a dinghy. Sanctuaries for birds and seals, these rocky ledges are often completely covered with living creatures, all of which break into raucous protest when neared. Here we found for the first time that there are occasional barrages of insects; but with a wind shift, the annoying gnat cloud will vanish just as quickly as it appeared. With the close proximity of seal and bird life on these upthrusting piles of granite (depicted on charts as islets) it was small wonder to find their accompanying parasites.

About 40 miles down the Gulf from Willard Bay some of the larger Midriff Islands loom into view. The second-largest of them all is 42-mile-long Angel de la Guarda, where Puerto Refugio at its northern extremity offers one of the best protected coves of any Gulf Island. We spent several days in the area, using Refugio as our base anchorage. Here sunrises and sunsets were especially violent in both color and aspect. It's an awesome and cruel-appearing place of great red slabs of jagged granite, occasionally

Elephant trees are indigenous to the Baja Peninsula and its offshore islands. This one rises from the rocky soil on Mejia Island, opposite Angel de la Guarda Island in the upper Gulf.

white-pocked with bird guano or with a thorned arm of cactus pointing toward the sky.

One morning we arose particularly early with color film in our cameras to record some of nature's artistry at dawn. Mejia Island, just north of our anchorage, was steeped in gold and crimson over its upper extremities, though bathed in blackness all around its base. The sight of it inspired one of us to write a picture caption: "A rugged range reflects its ramparts in a stunning mirror-sea." Some months later, however, when the picture was published, the magazine's less-inspired editor had changed the caption to read, simply: "Sunrise on Barren Mejia Island"— blunt testimony to the truth that 'beauty lies in the eyes of the beholder.' The total effect of a cruise to this region is similar:

for some it will generate the compulsion to return again and again; others may say it's a barren land, too harsh and lonely.

It was during a morning of exploration in our dinghy around the northern end of Angel de la Guarda Island that we noticed, for the first time in several days, that we actually had company— human company. Another 12-foot skiff was moving slowly around an outcropping, a fishing line dipped from its side.

"Maybe a native," Joe guessed. "Let's go over and ask him where the fishing's good."

As we neared the other boat a halloo hailed us: "Hey there, Jack and Carolyn, where'd you come from?"

We maneuvered our outboards closer and were surprised to see our good friends, Dr. Kenneth Norris and his wife, from Los Angeles. "We're here on a U.C.L.A. project," Ken told us, "studying the habits of some of this native fauna. There are a lot of chuckwalla or iguanas here on the Island. I've attached radio transmitters to some of the animals to find out where they travel, their diet and so forth." He told us the chuckwallas were equipped with sacks on the sides of their bodies which store water during the rainy season, for later consumption. During the long dry months they are able to drink salt water and convert it to fresh through their amazing built-in "conversion plant." We

A good airstrip and a protected anchorage at Bahia de Los Angeles are welcomed by sportfishermen from many miles distant.

made a date to meet again later aboard *Monsoon II,* to visit and hear more of the interesting findings of the University's ecology researchers.

Several days later we moved on to anchor in the protection of Bahia Los Angeles. Surrounded by 15 small islands and situated on the peninsula directly across from Angel de la Guarda's southerly end, Los Angeles Bay is a popular rendezvous for those flying in, coming by boat, or the few who brave the rough overland trail. A fresh-water spring, an adequate beach landing strip and the protection of its ample bay creates a pleasant stopover point for visitors. The Antero Diaz family have established a sport-fishing resort here which is steadily gaining popularity. Good food, and clean but unpretentious guest rooms are available with prior reservation. In an emergency one may be able to obtain food and lodging without previous notice but this should not be depended upon. As all supplies must be either flown in or brought by slow boat or slower overland transportation, it is obvious that the Diaz establishment must be operated by careful advance-planning of food and supplies.

Fifteen miles inland from Bahia Los Angeles and at an elevation of 1600 feet, lie the ruins of San Borja Mission. Built in 1760 by the Jesuits and native helpers, the Mission colony flourished for a few years, then dwindled and was finally abandoned in 1818. The community now consists of a few small ranches irrigated by several hot springs bubbling up from a palm grove. The great stone mission church still stands, but vandalism has taken its toll, in a literal sense, after its two ancient bells disappeared.

But while this inland settlement grows smaller, the Diaz village is in the making at the bayside. Fast charter boats are available for game fishing and about a hundred natives are otherwise employed in commercial turtle fishing. The only other human habitation in the area appears to be a small colony of Indians, some of whom we saw on tiny Raza Island, 36 miles south of Angel de la Guarda. When we approached the island and its cacophony of bird cries, we saw several of these timid fellows running across the island to hide with their loot of birds' eggs. On the shoreline of this flat, low island we found that a functional rock jetty had been built to permit a small boat's access into an inner bay. This we used to take our outboard into shallow water for closer inspection of the thousands of brooding gulls and terns, and to investigate the remnants of a rock fortress atop the island.

Several theories have been advanced as to the origin of these

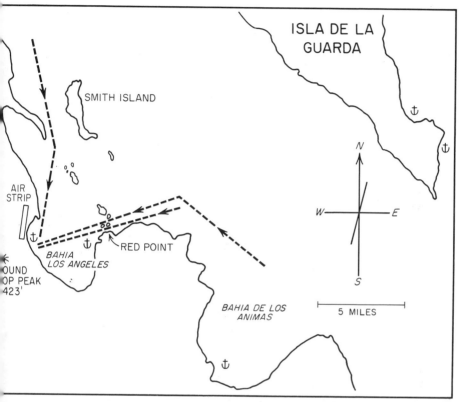

BAHIA DE LOS ANGELES
28 deg. 55 min. N. lat.
113 deg. 33 min. W. long.

Approach to this virtually land-locked 25-mile area harbor, from Canal de Ballenas, should be made between Red Point and two small islets or between the two small islets and a larger island of reddish color ½ mile north of the islets, when approaching from the southeast; or between Smith Island and the low-lying, narrow neck of land that projects southeastward from the mainland, if approaching from the northwest. The two channels close-by Red Point have 20 to 30 fathoms of depth. What appears to be a channel north of the large reddish island lying ½ mile northward of the two islets contains many sunken rocks with deep water close to them, and should not be used. When entering the harbor from the northwest, proceed well past the end of the narrow neck of land, because a shoal extends for some distance, before taking a heading to the anchorage. Some 15 islands or islets lie between Smith Island, Red Point and the bay. From the entrances, the bottom shoals gradually to the beach and anchorage can be made in 6 fathoms about ¼ mile offshore. Anchorage may also be taken just to the south of Red Point, in the Bay, and is often used during strong northeast or easterly winds that would make the anchorage off the resort an uncomfortable place to lie.

One of the many conical rock piles on Raza Island gives this Heermann Gull
a vantage point to guard his tiny plot of ground reserved for egg-hatching.

Thousands of Elegant Terns vie with gulls for claim-staking on 7-acre Raza Island during spring hatching season.

conical rock piles scattered across Raza Island. One theory holds that they are burial headstones. Another insists the stones were piled in heaps to make more usable ground space for birds to lay their (nestless) eggs. Still another belief is that the Yaqui Indians had built the stone fort for their protection during the Spanish Revolution of 1910 and that they piled the rock cones for handy hurling down on their aggressors in an attempt to hold their island camp. Whatever the facts, the only certainty at present is that birds have claimed Raza as their own private hatching grounds. The Indians we had seen stealing gull and tern eggs were some of the last of these predators. On May 30, 1964, President Lopez Mateos signed a decree which established Isla Raza as a Migratory Waterfowl Sanctuary. Thus these birds which were threatened with extinction will now be able to perpetuate their species, fight though they do for brooding-space on tiny Raza Island.

As Gulf waters had been completely calm for weeks on end, and their temperature held at a steady 75 degrees, we stopped frequently to swim or fish in the many tempting coves that indent the peninsula's contrasting shoreline; Las Animas Bay, then San Francisquito Bay. The latter, the four of us agreed, is one of our favorite anchorages. It is a bay about 1 mile in width, with a smaller bay off its eastern shore, extending another ¼ mile into the low-lying hills.

In mentioning San Francisquito Bay it might be well to state clearly and definitely at the outset that there is *no* fresh water available at this cove. During the last four years there have been several published reports that potable water could be taken on from this location. Obviously someone erred in the first published guide, and subsequent writers copied the erroneous report without having investigated the true situation. It is true that San

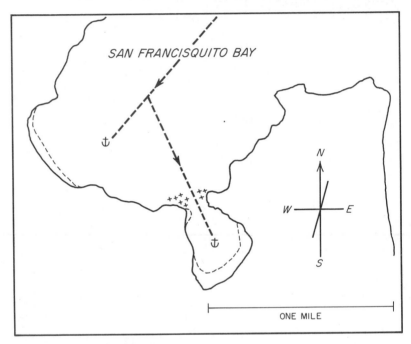

SAN FRANCISQUITO BAY
28 deg. 50 min. N. lat.
112 deg. 52 min. W. long.

Approaches to the 1-mile-wide San Francisquito Bay are deep, with no outlying rocks. The entrance to the Bay ranges from 10 to 20 fathoms in depth, and gradually shoals toward the beach at the southwest end of the Bay. Within as little as 500 yards, there are between 3 and 5 fathoms of water. Holding is excellent, with a clean sand bottom. Smaller craft can anchor in the smaller bay that opens off the southeast side of the main bay. Care should be exercised when entering it because rocks or ledges extend from either side of the entrance and restrict the entrance to a channel of approximately 100 yards in width. Within the smaller bay there are from 2 to 4 fathoms of water up to within 150 yards of the shoreline.

Francisquito Cove is quite often used by small boats as a refueling station, but both gasoline and water put aboard there are from containers previously ordered and brought to the site by commercial or fishing boats, just for this purpose. There *is* well water at El Barril, a tiny rancho about 12 miles south of Bahia San Francisquito but these wells are privately owned and one would of course need permission to draw water from this source.

Despite its lack of facilities, however, San Francisquito Bay is a picturesque and sheltered anchorage. Its long, white beaches are a delight for the shell collector—pink and white murex, Gulf spiny murex, conchs and variegated auger shells, beside many we couldn't name—all were scattered with eye-pleasing abandon along the strand. At one end of the beach we discovered a high pile of shucked pearl-oyster shells, indicating some pearling still exists. Near the shell pile was another mound of broken greenish rock laced intermittently with a deeper blue-green vein. This darker strata of semi-precious chryscolla had been mostly removed from the dross by quarry workers and presumably shipped away for sale to gem polishers. It was obvious that both fishermen and miners had brought their separating chores to the beach, to work at their trade in leisure and peaceful surroundings.

Joe and Sue were our fish providers. (For some unaccountable reason, we don't care to fish—but are always glad to help eat the catch.) They came back to the ship one afternoon with two fine cabrillas and a surprising announcement:

"You'll never guess,'" they called, "we are all invited ashore for cocktails this evening!"

Inasmuch as we hadn't seen another soul in the three days we had spent at San Francisquito—not even a native fisherman, we laughed. "What's the punch line?"

"I mean it," Joe said. "Two couples in campers just drove in to the smaller bay and set up their awnings and stuff and asked us 'where are all the people?' "

"I told them 'we' were all the people. So they asked us over for martinis. I said we would bring the ice and they seemed surprised that we would have ice on our boat."

We didn't think of it at the time, but that would have made a picture: Eight people sitting around a contrived patio near the campers, tinkling glasses in hand—in the midst of the wilds —"Martinis on the Bush!"

They were pleasant folk. We listened with interest to their story of their dusty, rough drive from the border, averaging at

best 20 miles a day. They were headed for La Paz. Their campers
were filled to brimming with as many home comforts as were possible to make transportable. But all we could think of was: what
a way to go! Later it was revealed that they were not boat-
minded. Undoubtedly they pitied us our travels at sea.

There are several quiet anchorages below San Francisquito
before reaching Santa Rosalia, the one breakwatered port on the
peninsula's eastern shore: San Raphael Bay, San Carlos and many
others nameless. We looked into them all with our usual time
out for fishing and swimming. By now our foursome aboard
found ourselves following the wildlife's habit of early to bed and
early to rise. Dawn was not to be missed; dawn, literally and
emotionally a moving sight. From absolute stillness and with
first light only a loom in the east, there's a sudden splash. A gull
cries, awakening chittery land birds to voice. Another splash and
more birds shriek. Skies take on light and color as all the seascape
turns to action, rising in a small tumultuous crescendo of whirl-
ing, diving, feeding, crying. The sun bursts over a far horizon.
Its heat distills a fresh, rich scent of desert and tideland. It's day.
And the birds' and fishes' breakfast frenzy subsides. Our cue to
start the morning coffee.

Hours before reaching Santa Rosalia, the brown plume of
smoke from the towering chimney of their copper-smelter could
be seen. We stopped at this port only because we had been told
we might take on water here. But when the Port Captain told us
THEY boiled it before use, we agreed that it was preferable to
ration our remaining half-tankful aboard ship until we reached
La Paz, whose water supply is both pure and soft. Beyond that,
Santa Rosalia is a good supply stop, provided that one can negotiate its precarious under-the-dock ladder to get ashore. We were
interested in a short tour of this historic copper mining community, inhabited primarily by French descendants. It is not a pretty
place due to its industry, heat and barren surroundings, but its
lacks are far outweighed by its hospitable and friendly citizenry.
Joe and the Port Captain found an immediate mutual bond: they
were both amateur radio operators. It was hard to tear them
apart from their "ham" session. But we had shopping to do. We
bought eggs, fresh fruit and tomatoes, excellent bread at their
French Panaderia (bakery) and a half-dozen cans of delicious
Mexican mangoes.

As mentioned before, the harbor of Santa Rosalia has a breakwater for protection, but inside there are submerged wrecked

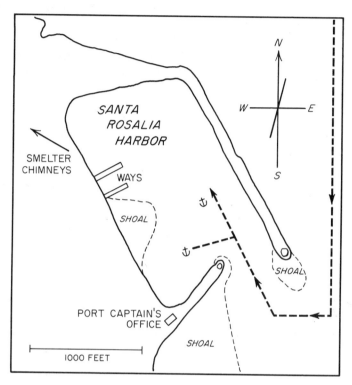

SANTA ROSALIA HARBOR
27 deg. 20 min. N. lat.
112 deg. 16 min. W. long.

The artificial harbor of Santa Rosalia is formed by the only breakwaters of any harbor in Baja California, excepting Ensenada. It is 1½ miles north-westward of Santa Agueda Point, which should be given at least ½-mile berth because of shoals. Similarly, the southeast end of the seaward breakwater should be given a wide berth because of shoaling that is not shown on available charts. Lights are shown on the ends of the breakwater and the mole, but a night-time approach to the harbor is not recommended. Once inside the entrance, care should be exercised in picking a spot to anchor because of unmarked piles, wrecks and shoals that exist within the harbor. Vessels of up to 20-foot draft are accommodated within the harbor, and are frequently alongside the wharf at the northwest end of the harbor. Anchoring close-by the wharf built on the southeast mole provides easier access to the Port Captain's office, where taxis can be obtained for the short ride to the community.

ships and remains of old pilings, none of which are visible from the surface. A daytime entrance, and movement at slow bell are indicated. There will usually be someone on the dock or aboard a commercial boat to suggest where to anchor and where the Port Captain may be found for Customs clearance.

We stopped briefly at San Marcos Island, southeast of Santa Rosalia and opposite San Lucas Cove on the peninsula. Although there is nothing of importance ashore other than its industrial

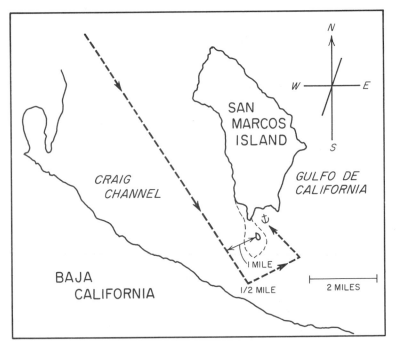

SAN MARCOS ISLAND, LOBOS ROCK ANCHORAGE
27 deg. 11 min. N. lat.
112 deg. 05 min. W. long.

When approaching this anchorage from Santa Rosalia, or other northwestern points, it is necessary to take a heading along the west side of the island that clears Lobos Rock by approximately 1 mile, and continue past it until the mainland shoreline of Craig Channel is approximately ½ mile distant. This is to give a wide berth to a shoal area extending southward from Lobos Rock. Course can then be changed to the northeast and later to the northwest, heading toward the prominent bluffs. Anchorage in 2 to 4 fathoms, good holding sand, ¼ mile from the Island shore provides good protection from northwest prevailing winds. Tenders can normally be beached in the bay although it is a rock beach, and if any swell is coming into the bay it is better to anchor the tender a short distance offshore and wade into the beach.

gypsum-mining operation, we were anxious to make another attempt to photograph some eagles on their nests that we had seen on a previous visit. As we neared the island's southern anchorage just east of Lobos Rock, one eagle did appear at home on his lofty nest perched atop a steep rock pinnacle. But just as I had the bird within camera range, off he flew, disappearing as quickly as his counterpart on the American dollar.

Aside from the gypsum operation on San Marcos, the surrounding waters are the scene of another major Gulf industry—turtle fishing. Despite the turtle's size and weight (50 to 250 pounds) he proves an elusive prey. Hunted only in the dark of the moon when his phosphorescent trail can be detected, the hunters work in pairs, one paddling silently while his partner stands in the canoa's bow, harpoon-spear poised, ready for hurling the moment his practiced eye spots his quarry. Following a direct hit, there is a splashing scramble before the great beast is brought into the boat. Turtle meat ("caguama" on the Mexican menu) is a singular delicacy, far superior to Mexican beef.

When leaving San Marcos Island's southern anchorage it is wise to plot a course well to the east to avoid the large shoal area which extends south and west of the Island. When the shoal area is at least 1 mile astern, one may then safely swing to starboard to point toward Chivato Point and Santa Inez Bay, for an anchorage at Mulege, on the northwest extremity of Concepcion Bay.

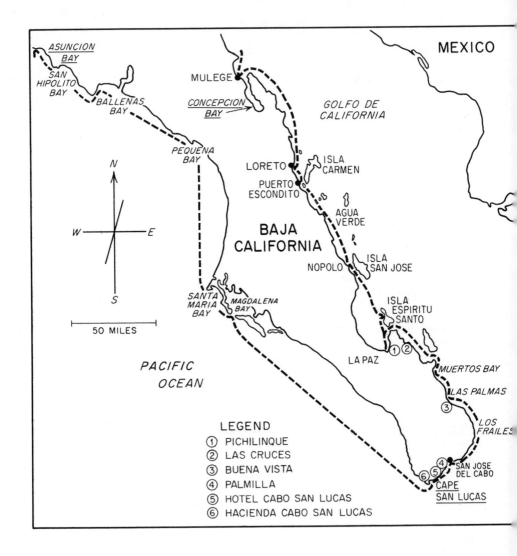

CHAPTER 3

Concepcion Bay to La Paz

Mulege and adjoining Concepcion Bay, near the 27th parallel, is rapidly becoming the Gulf's most popular mid-peninsula resort. Four good airstrips welcome those flying in for fishing and hunting, and there are ample choices of protected anchorages for the boatman. (See chart.) This is a favored fishing area for trailer-size boats coming across from the mainland and for sport fishing craft kept year-around in Mexico. From Guaymas on the mainland it's an 85-mile cruise across the Gulf, and many make this run to Mulege in four to five hours.

On this particular afternoon we found the anchorage between Prieta and Sombrerito Point rather untenable in the afternoon northeast breeze. So we chose instead to take *Monsoon II* into the protection of Concepcion Bay and return to Mulege in our dinghy. Sheltered by low-lying hills with fairly dense vegetation, Concepcion Bay extends 22 miles inland and varies from 2 to 5 miles in width. We anchored in 5 fathoms in a small bite on the southwesterly side, about 8 miles inside the Bay, and then wasted no time in launching the dinghy.

Joe and Sue looked sad. For them it was their last anchorage before having to pack away their fishing gear and prepare to fly home from Mulege. This was a prearranged "exchange stop" where we would presently have other guests flying down to join us for the balance of our cruise to La Paz. The four of us had had such a pleasant six weeks of cruising together that we, too, were regretting that their vacation was nearly over.

It took nearly an hour to return to Mulege in our little 7½ h.p. outboard but since we all agreed "What's the hurry?", we relaxed on our cushions and enjoyed the passing shoreside scenery while Joe and Sue took turns trolling.

It is only after rounding Sombrerito Point (which looks like a huge hat topped with a lighthouse) and turning inland up the

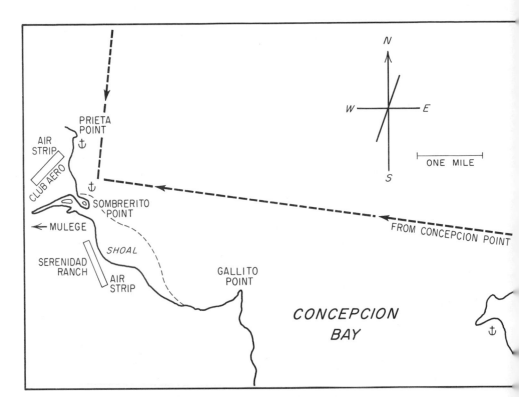

MULEGE ANCHORAGE IN CONCEPCION BAY
26 deg. 53 min. N. lat.
111 deg. 58 min. W. long.

The approaches to Mulege Anchorage are clear, and the bottom gradually shoals to the beach. Anchorage is normally taken between Prieta Point and Sombrerito Point, in depths of 4 or more fathoms, keeping Sombrerito Point about ¼ mile distant and to the southwest. A shoal extends off Sombrerito Point to the southeast as indicated on the chart. Once anchored, passage can be made with a tender up to the small docks on the banks of the Rosalia River. During high tide, local fishermen will take boats of up to 25 and 30 feet in length to the first of the docks, on the inside of Sombrerito Point, but shallow water and sand bars above that point restrict travel to outboard-powered boats. With care in picking the deeper water—ranging from 2 to 5 feet in depth—passage can be made up the river for 2 miles to the community of Mulege, through tropic tree-lined channels. During any degree of northeast or easterly winds the anchorage is uncomfortable, and anchorage should be taken further into Concepcion Bay, along either its southwesterly or northeasterly shores, depending on the wind conditions.

river, that the full vivid impact strikes one—of Mulege, green as the Emerald City of Oz! Through a thick tangle of palms, mango and palo verde trees, little ranchos are visible at intervals all along the river edge. Snook and pargo jumped in the river. Natives were bringing their horses and burros to bathe and drink. We wondered why all of Baja residents were not drawn here to live at Mulege with its miracle of fresh flowing water.

High above the village and above the river's dam, the ancient Mission of Santa Rosalia de Mulege sits alone, casting its benediction down upon this settlement spawned from the river's succor. Across from the Mission stands the bleached-white structural bones of Mulege's Federal prison. Its handful of prisoners work at various trades on surrounding ranchos or in town by day, and return at sundown to retire behind the locked gates of Carcel de Cananea—their part-time prison.

Date-growing is Mulege's principal industry. The Jesuits planted the date palms along the river banks early in 1700, when the Mission was first established. Since that time the groves have flourished, despite the many reverses of both this and other Baja Missions. Now flourishing too is tourism for tropical Mulege. Besides the small "Hacienda" hotel in town, there are two Gulf-fronting hotels: "Club Aero de Mulege," situated on a hill just north of the river, and "Serenidad," a beachside establishment. Each has its own airstrip, restaurant, pleasant hotel rooms and sport fishing boats for charter.

We stopped first at Club Aero's riverside small-boat landing, and walked up the hill for a view from the Club. A putting green and an inviting swimming pool center the hotel's well-tended gardens. Inside the air-conditioned lounge a group of exotic birds could be heard twittering in their outdoor aviary facing the bar. The bartender was busy with his radio, talking on the Unicom frequency to an incoming airplane.

". . . wind's from the east, about 10 m.p.h.," he said, "we'll have a jeep waiting for you at the airstrip."

The pilot's voice came back: "Mulege Radio from N 259 . . . roger; we'll want two rooms, please, for a party of four. And, hey there, what's for dinner?"

The bartender laughed. "Camarones, Senior. The shrimpers are in! Mulege off."

This is the comfortable and informal atmosphere at Club Aero. There are no telephones, no newspapers—yet VHF radio is in continuous operation, linking this small oasis to the planes coming in or passing high in the sky.

The village of Mulege lies 2 miles inland from Club Aero, and as we found the river too shallow that afternoon to take our outboard all the way upstream, we took a "taxi" instead. The car's young driver opened the glove compartment and proudly produced a small pulp-paper Spanish/English grammar book. "I study English," he told us. "Please you talk in English to me."

We were pleasantly surprised at how well he spoke. After examining his book we were even further surprised. On each page was a picture of an object captioned with an English term. One such illustration showed a coat hanger; its caption—"perch." It reminded us of the two separate definitions shown in our own Spanish dictionary of the word "cochero." Its first meaning is "coachman"; the second, "easily boiled." Indeed, books do help one learn. People-to-people association proves a more functional key.

We spent the balance of the afternoon talking with the villagers and taking pictures of the area around Mulege and the Mission. We dined at Club Aero that evening while visiting with some of their guests. The party of four who had recently flown in told us they were on their way down to the Cape. Three tanned and bearded men sat at a table nearby, discussing their overland jeep drive down the peninsula. Others were boat owners, here for a few days of fishing. "Go to Coyote Cove if you want butter clams," we were told. And our new friend drew us a rough chart of other interesting anchorages in Concepcion Bay.

And clams there were at Coyote. We didn't know there could be such an abundance of these tasty cockles. No rakes nor shovels were necessary as are often needed for such collecting; it was merely a matter of scooping them up by hand from their shallow sandy beds at low-tide level. Back aboard ship, we prepared dinner—a banquet that evening: clam cocktail, sivichi made from fresh cabrilla fillets, local vine-ripened tomatoes, langusta dipped in melted garlic-butter and fresh papaya for dessert. In Concepcion Bay, our ship's supplies of canned and frozen foods experienced few inroads.

Later we took *Monsoon II* the length of the Bay, charting its depths as we cruised. At the far end, on shore, there's a dense forest of cactus "trees," ranging up to 20 feet high. From the natives we learned there are great herds of deer living in the

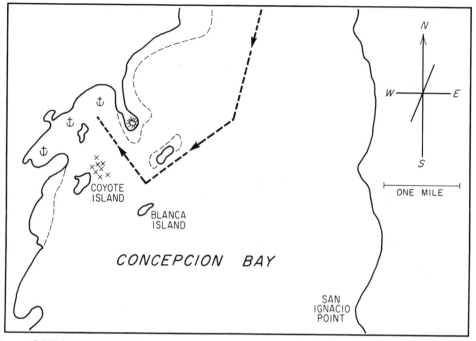

CONCEPCION BAY
26 deg. 45 min. N. lat.
111 deg. 53 min. W. long.

When proceeding southeastward down Concepcion Bay, it is well to maintain a course mid-channel because of the shoals extending toward it along
most of the southwestern side of the Bay, for the first 9 miles from Sombrerito Point. Coyote Cove is a well-protected anchorage from any winds,
with sand bottom and sand beaches. On the northwestern side of it is a
lagoon, near the mouth of which is excellent clam digging. Approach to
the Bay should be taken by rounding the islet that is southeast of the prominent 200-foot high cone that marks the northeast side of the Bay, then turning to the northwest. Coyote Island has a prominent group of rocks extending
from it to the northeast. Between the rocks and the 200-foot-high cone there
is from 5 to 10 fathoms of water. The road from Mulege to La Paz skirts
along the shoreline of the Bay.

area, though how they forage through the spiney cactus branches
was hard to imagine.

All too soon it was D for Depature day for the Kellys: but not
before a farewell party on the beach. Three couples flew down
from Los Angeles in an Aero Commander belonging to a pilot
friend of Joe's, who was to fly them home. We swam and ex-

plored the many beaches along Concepcion's westerly shore, and our new guests' white skins rapidly reddened. The men built a cooking fire on the beach, and after several dinghy trips back and forth with supplies we commenced our clambake. (However, the main course was clam Bordelaise instead of baked clams. Someone forgot to bring the wine from the ship, a necessary ingredient for our entree. Someone else substituted bourbon. The clam mélange had never tasted better!)

Baja California's oldest Mission, at Loreto.

By moonrise we were all still in our swim suits, eating awhile and swimming awhile, in the soft, warm waters of the Bay. Storm and strife of world affairs seemed as distant as the stars—light-years away.

A few days later we weighed anchor and headed down the Gulf for Loreto, the site of Baja's oldest Mission. This is about a 70-mile cruise, interspersed with several small anchorages along the way. Good protection from the north may be found just south of Pulpito Point and Mangles Point. Only shallow-draft boats should attempt the approximate 800-foot-wide passage between Coronado Island and the peninsula, as this is generally shoal water with rocky islets, only some of which are visible. The safest course lies outside of Coronado Island and then on a more southerly heading to leave the north end of Carmen Island to port.

On shore, the towering mountain range of Sierra de la Giganta looms ever higher against a deep blue sky. On the Gulf horizon an early afternoon mirage builds a fantasy in pale ochre—a strange tan island with squared-off vertical cliffs. It hangs there in the distance, a fair height above water, resting on nothing whatsoever but air. Binoculars only magnify the apparition. Our charts deny its existence.

Loreto is a Port of Entry, necessitating Clearance with their Port Captain. Although this area is actually open roadstead, the best anchorage is about ¾ mile south of the Mission Church dome, visible above a line of palm trees, and ¼ mile off a pier serving the Flying Sportsmen Lodge. We visited briefly with our friend, Ed Tabor, owner of the Lodge, and were interested to see the many new developemnts surrounding his grounds. A new airstrip has been hewn out of the thornbush, back of the hotel; additions made to the main buildings; a vegetable garden and extensive landscaping added, since our last visit.

Our first cruise to Loreto in 1950 coincided with the grand opening of Flying Sportsmen Lodge. Natives were then excavating for their Gulf-fronting swimming pool, using sharpened turtle shells for spades. The last tile was being placed on the patio floor and supplies of food and drink were being carried into the new kitchen. A fiesta was to start that night, destined to last well over two days. Families were coming in by horse and burro-back from ranchos miles distant. It was a memorable night of music and dancing, no more enjoyed by the natives than by our own group from *Monsoon*—prize winners for having traveled the greatest distance to help officially "open" the Lodge.

The town of Loreto lies about 1 mile north of the Lodge resort. Although the church, with its great bells brought in the early 1700's from Spain, has been restored since a onetime earthquake, the community itself remains little changed through the years. Only the palms and vivid flowering trees were larger, casting longer shadows on hot white streets and dusty dwellings. It was Sunday, and a baseball game was in progress near the village. We watched the game awhile and later, on our return to the beach, visited a neighboring tienda to buy more of their fine tomatoes, some melons and a few hot chili peppers.

Although *Sailing Directions* issue only a brief report of Puerto Escondito (Hidden Harbor) this anchorage 15 miles southeast of Loreto is considered the only completely all-weather anchorage in the Gulf. Shallow-draft boats can go beyond the first large bay through a shallow channel which opens into a mangrove-rimmed inner bay. Here oysters abound, some on bordering rocks and others clinging to the mangrove roots at low-tide level. Towering more than 4,000 feet above Puerto Escondito are massive twin peaks of the Giganta Range, appearing as sentinels guarding the

In the landlocked harbor of Puerto Escondito (Hidden Harbor) the Kellys pry off rock oysters while Jack tends the dinghy.

Bay. Recently a portion of the anchorage has been dredged and a pier constructed, in preparation for the day when building commences of another luxury resort hotel and adjoining airstrip.

As we lay at anchor that evening, listening to the nightly orchestration of mourning doves cooing in their strange drum-like cadence, our thoughts turned to memories of our first visit to Puerto Escondito; of the incident of Romero and the black pearls.

Romero was an Indian—maybe 50, maybe 70 years old; it was hard to tell. We saw him first in the anchorage paddling his dugout canoe piled high with dried salt-shark. "Buenos tardes, senor," we called, and invited him to tie his canoe alongside and come aboard. We were interested in his cargo and where he was taking it. Romero explained he was on his way to Loreto to sell the load of shark meat. "And how long will it take you to paddle that distance?" we inquired. "Two, maybe three days," Romero answered in his soft, grave voice. "Depends on the winds."

We were heading that way in *Monsoon* the next morning, we told him. "Why not let us hoist your canoe and its load aboard our ship? You ride with us."

Although we did not have power winches, we did have sturdy block and tackle astern for lifting our heavy New England dory. At first Romero demurred. It would be much trouble for us. "No trouble at all" we insisted. At last it was settled. He would spend the night with us, and we would bring his shark-load and canoe aboard in the morning. We offered Romero a spare bunk in the fo'castle, but he insisted in sleeping on deck.

At daybreak, our guest Stan Vine and Romero started hoisting the loaded dugout canoe, but at no time had we realized the tremendous weight of Romero's boat! Even with all hands lending their weight on the lines, the load came up only inches at a time. "We should have towed it!" someone finally gasped. And I still don't know why we didn't. Perhaps it was feared we would swamp it. Whatever the reason, no one wanted to back down on a promise. The canoe with its load was finally secured athwartship an hour later.

In less than two hours we were anchored at Loreto, and prepared to lower Romero's dugout. "Una momento, senores" he said. From a pocket in his much-patched shirt Romero drew forth a tiny packet to display two lovely black pearls. He extended them to Stan's wife, Donna, and myself. "Por ustedes y con muchas gracias" (for you and with many thanks) he told us. Donna and I were overcome. We thought at first he wanted to sell them, but our friend insisted they were gifts—we must take them. The pearls, though not especially large, would nevertheless have purchased many needed supplies for Romero and his family. We wanted so much to have him keep them. But one look at the Indian's expressive eyes was our directive. To do other than graciously accept Romero's gift would have been unthinkable. And through the years, we have found such deportment the rule rather than the exception. These are the caballeros, the proud gentlemen of Mexico.

About 10 miles south of Puerto Escondito, Agua Verde Bay is another secluded and quiet anchorage. Its waters are sheltered by outlying reefs and islands, and its shores are kept green by springs which seep down from the 2- to 4000-foot mountain peaks overshadowing the Bay. The best anchorage lies midway between Point Pasquel and a 350-foot peak to the south, off the beach in about 4 to 10 fathoms. There is a small settlement ashore and a new school for the children. The bay also serves as access to a few ranches inland.

Another 35 miles southeast, opposite the midpoint of San Jose Island, is Nopolo Point. Just to the west of the point is another palm-green oasis surrounding a small anchorage. Natives call it simply "Nopolo" (Nŏp′-a-low). H.O. #84 scarcely mentions the bay, but it is a favored anchorage of those who know the Gulf well and enjoy shoregoing at more primitive settlements. A several-generation family of about 40 people with their cats, dogs, chickens and goats comprise the community whose life is dedicated to fishing. This is one of the very few native families on the peninsula whose women-folk take active part along with the men in fishing. This handsome group, of French and Yaqui Indian ancestry, appeared delighted to have visitors, and insisted we come ashore to inspect their tropical home-setting. Although we found their dialect quite unlike the usual peninsula language, we were able (mainly through sign language) to understand the general trend of their conversation. Some of the women pointed with pride to the handmade flower baskets decorating the eves of their thatched-roof porch. A variety of suspended cans cascaded wild flowers and ferns, adding a little touch of elegance to this community so obviously proud of its rare peninsula luxury— proximity to fresh spring water.

Before entering La Paz Harbor, we stayed a few days to swim and snorkel at lovely Espiritu Santo and La Partida Islands and their many blue-green coves. Here the beaches are of finely-pul-

Strange rock formations, sculptured by wind and water, mark the eastern side of Espiritu Santo and La Partida Islands.

verized white coral—which to walk on, barefoot, feels like treading on talcum. At high tide one can take a dinghy between these islands, the winding channel festooned with rock oysters, clams and crabs. Puffer fish, bat rays, tiny electric bluefish, red snapper and now and then a turtle, moved in calm detachment before our face-plates. On an outcropping of rock, armies of spindle-legged crabs would pause to watch us fearfully with their hyper-thyroid eyes.

Of the entire two months spent in the Gulf this trip, there was only one night of violent wind when we felt need of anchor watch. This occurred in an unnamed cove on the east side of Espiritu Santo Island, where a magnificent arc of beach nestled at the base of a thousand-foot rocky cliff. (The geographical setting itself should have warned us, that calm afternoon we beachcombed and swam around the shore.) This was an area un-surpassed for snorkling. Massive schools of fish moved just under the surface, only a few yards off the beach. We stared at them through our faceplates while they in turn moved closer to stare back at us, completely unafraid. We thought, "This must be the feeling of raptures of the deep." Time passed unnoticed, so absorbed were we with the changing spectrum about us—people and fishes mingling as if we were all of a species. It was nearly sunset when reluctantly we tore ourselves away from our afternoon's enchantment, and returned aboard ship.

About ten that night a 50-knot wind came suddenly slamming down on us from over the cliffs, roaring like a cyclone along the granite walls. In all probability, this cove was unnamed simply because it was unused—by cautious natives. Our anchor held throughout the onslaught, but by morning "no-name harbor" had lost our interest. We weighed anchor and headed southwest for Prieta Point and the entrance channel to La Paz.

CHAPTER 4

La Paz to Cape San Lucas

On a southwesterly course we crossed San Lorenzo Channel in early afternoon. The sun-soaked Sea of Cortez glinted blue and gold in sparkling reflection from sky and shore. Abeam Diablo Point our heading bent southeasterly, to leave Lobos Rock and Lobos Island close to port. From the southern end of San Juan Nepomezeino Island, marking the entrance to Pichilinque Harbor, we turned on our depth recorder. This is where shallower water commences, with depths varying from 2 to 5 fathoms. At Prieta Point, marking the La Paz channel entrance, we reduced speed to just above steerage way, proceeding slowly through the poorly marked channel.

Monsoon II draws 7 feet, and in many places beside the channel, shifting sandbars shoal to less than our draft. In earlier days, cement range-markers on the hills were used to negotiate the channel. Today, unfortunately, the ranges only approximately indicate the channel's deepest water. The best guide of all, however, is the sight of a medium-draft pleasure boat temporarily stuck in the sand, listing, dead in the water—a too-common sight, unfortunately, when visiting boats have tried to negotiate this channel at night.

We passed the beautiful white mansion that La Paz citizens built for ex-President Aleman; then the bathing beach at El Coromuel; and finally moved in to the anchorage at La Paz, the 450-year-old Capitol of Baja's Southern Territory. Along the harbor waterfront's malecon, buildings shone between palms and pina-blanca trees and the fire colors of bougainvillea cascaded down faded plaster walls. Today La Paz has a population of 30,000 people, many cars on good intercity highways, and an airport serving jet flights. She is becoming a sophisticated little city and we are glad for her economic growth. But with some small pangs I missed the sight and sound of La Paz 20 years ago when windmills clanged softly through drowsy afternoons, and the only traffic sounds on cobbled streets were horse hooves clopping. In those days, La Paz identified with her name—"peace."

The most recent boon for the non-boat-owning tourist is the advent of the 360-foot commercial tour-ship *M.S. La Paz* plying the Gulf, from Mazatlan on the mainland, to La Paz and return. With accommodations for 375 people and 115 vehicles, the ferry is well equipped, with a restaurant and theatre aboard. The trans-Gulf cruise takes about 16 hours one way, at a speed of 17 knots, thus opening the southern tip of the Peninsula to an increasing number of visitors beyond those who fly in or come by their own boats.

However one comes into La Paz, there are many comfortable (and some very beautiful) hotels and restaurants for his vacation comfort. Fast fishing boats are available for charter, and the nearly surfless expanse of Coromuel Beach is inviting for sunning and swimming. La Paz Harbor is a protected anchorage, but care should be used in anchoring to insure holding in the 2- to 6-knot currents occurring during tidal changes. During winter and early spring months there are apt to be strong northerly winds in the harbor, at which time most boats move to Pichilinque's all-weather protection. This is the docking site for the trans-Gulf ferry.

The day following our arrival we launched our dinghy for a trip ashore. It seemed good to walk again in early morning on freshly washed sidewalks, shade- and sun-dappled. A half-square beyond the malecon is the cool, thick-walled office of our long-time friend, Senor Fernando Chacon, agent and aficionado of the boating fraternity. Our basic mission was the ritual of Customs papers, but first we inquired of each other's families, discussed the growth of the city, and talked of eventful highlights transpired since a former meeting. There is no hurry; there *can* be no hurry here.

Later we took a cab out to the fringe of town for fresh bread, still warm from its outdoor brick oven. Groceries and sundries may be had from the old farm market with its scores of stalls— eggs, fresh fruits, vegetables, staples, clothes, leather goods, stalks of sugar cane, live poultry or newly butchered cuts of pork or beef. Each commodity emits its own aroma. (Food to eat, and food for thought!) The farm market has more color than the new supermarket south of town. Except for foreign labels on its shelf

A portion of La Paz harbor. Foreground, the noted author and fishing authority, Ray Cannon.

goods, the super-mercado is a duplicate of our own at home—even to chromed shopping carts and turnstiles.

One day we took a taxi out of La Paz up to the old Triunfo gold and silver mines. A long day's journey into yesteryear—to El Triunfo and to San Antonio's mines, which in 1862 were expected to bring unlimited riches to the territory. However, transportation from mine to harbor proved too great a problem; native workers were neither experienced nor dependable; and during the first years of these mining ventures, all was turmoil in the Mexican Government.* This combination of adversities left El Triunfo and San Antonio virtually ghost towns, their empty, crumbling buildings rimmed 'round with green-gold torote, wild bougainvillea and red flowering octillo. Gaunt cattle roam the

---

* See *Exploration in Lower California 1868* by J. Ross Browne, Harper & Bros. (reprinted by *Arizona Silhouettes*, Tucson, Arizona).

thickets for food, blobs of cactus on their sad faces. Overhead the vulture hovers, a black-winged cross against the blue.

But somehow a few families manage to wrest a livelihood from their tiny ranchos, their goat herds and poultry flocks. We lunched in one such casa in a small but tidy dining room surrounded on all sides with the latticed green of tropical foliage. Our host and his family appeared happy and content as we visited. They spoke no English, and we only moderate Spanish. As is usual in these circumstances, there is always the mistaken phrase, the fumbling for explanation, gesticulations and finally mutual laughter. Laughter at ourselves—humans with the same needs and desires, all with tongues for voice but withal, this ridiculous lack of communication. We exit laughing.

It was dusk when we arrived back at the harbor from our day-long drive in the mountain mining country. And laughter again surrounded us while we loaded our dinghy to return to our anchored ship. I had gathered such a load of rock specimens from the mine area—quartz, fools' gold, obsidian and any other stones I'd found that were colored, or that sparkled. The native boat-boys were convulsed. "Look," they cried to one another. "Look, mira, this lady likes our *rocks!* She takes our old stones with her!" Indeed, how "loco" could one be?

A curious thing happened next day. Our son Gordon had been fishing, and brought back several cabrilla. The fish lay there, dead, I assumed, in the bottom of the dinghy. When I started to pick one up, it made one convulsive movement and bit my hand. It was only a small puncture and I thought little of it. But a few minutes later I felt completely drugged. For the next three hours I slept so soundly I had to be forcibly awakened. We have since wondered if this was a true cabrilla (which is not presumed to be poisonous) or perhaps some mutation or crossbred, dressed in conventional cabrilla fins. Two big mugs of double-strength coffee eventually cleared my sleep-fogged brain, and there were no untoward aftereffects. But I keep wondering about the chemical formula emitted by that biting fish. For insomniacs, this extract might provide an excellent sleeping potion.

There are a variety of short trips which one may take out of La Paz, by boat, plane or taxi. The closest resort is less than a ten-minute flight across the southeast coast to Rancho de Las Cruces. Other, slightly longer trips bring one into Rancho Buena Vista, to Bahia de Las Palmas, or to the several newer resort hotels at Cape San Lucas. For those with limited vacation time,

A school of small whales which has swum ashore near La Paz. Scientists are unable to explain why the sea mammals do this. Hundreds have been known to die in this seemingly senseless act.

the airplane has been a special boon here in Baja's Southern Territory. But reservations, especially during the winter season, are a necessity. Both Christmas and Easter holidays are particularly popular vacation intervals in these Cape resorts because of their fine weather and splendid fishing opportunities. (See fishing calendar—appendix.) For the sailor, however, blessed with a boat and a little more time available, there is always the happy assurance of self-sufficiency, his bed and board being forever with him.

Since La Paz is the last supply depot of any consequence for those circumnavigating the peninsula, one stocks his galley at that harbor to last a week or more during the run up the Pacific side of the coast. (However, there is pure spring water available at Las Palmas, and both fuel and water at Cape San Lucas cannery dock.)

The distance from La Paz to the Cape's extremity is approximately 125 miles, and with no particular hazards along the route, and five (rare for the peninsula) navigational lights, it may be safely cruised by night. However, there are many pleasant anchorages to explore, enticing most boatmen to make this leg in easy stages. Muertos Bay provides excellent protection although there are no facilities ashore—only a vacant warehouse building, originally used for storing salt for export shipment.

Las Palmas Bay, a few hours' cruising time south, is another tiny green oasis, sprouting out from an otherwise barren vista of low, rolling hills studded with cactus and thornbush. A freshwater spring at Las Palmas produces a small grove of palm trees and attracts the inevitable rancho, a few crops and a resort hotel. The latter is an inviting low, rambling structure, with thatched-roof patios surrounding a swimming pool and out-of-doors bar. Las Palmas is noted for its Mexican chuck-wagon-styled dinners with an atmosphere informal and relaxed.

After rounding Punta Arena there comes the unmistakable feeling of approaching ocean swells, at first gradual, then an increasing awareness of the open Pacific. Los Frailes Bay, south of Punta Arena, is another good anchorage protected from north and northwest winds, but offering no shoreside facilities. It does possess a long white arc of empty beach and several rocky outcroppings, offering the skin or Scuba diver another underwater paradise for exploration or fishing.

A little way south of Los Frailes, the Cape's rocky contour bends westward around Punta Gorda, southwest of which is a navigational light marking the onetime commercial port of San Jose del Cabo. This village, situated about two miles inland from the open-roadstead "port," was the peninsula's major trading post from the 16th to the 19th century. But now few vessels attempt to lie at anchor there. Surge is constant, even in relatively windless weather. Breakers crash unceasingly against its uninviting shore. The town site is best approached by taxi, overland from Cape San Lucas or from La Paz. A newly built road connecting La Paz and Cape San Lucas passes through San Jose del Cabo. The route is rich with spectacular scenery as it goes over mountain passes or along the rugged shoreline.

This is the valley of the San Jose River, which is nearly dry at times, although occasionally a raging torrent during a summer's rainy season. From a dry, cactus-ridden ridge overlooking the valley, the great swath of green below appears as unlikely as any mirage at sea. With the first trickle of water, the wastelands explode into a veritable jungle—tone on tone of leafy green. Fruit trees, sugar cane, artichokes, bananas and all manner of tropical foodstuffs proliferate the length of this 30-mile valley, which tumbles down toward the ocean. The Mission, established in 1730, was first built high in the arroyo some 20 miles inland. Later it was moved to its present site at San Jose del Cabo where it still stands, little weathered by the years. It's a serene little community, with strongly built structures and great wide streets —reminiscent of an earlier-day, large population when its exports of cheeses and panoche were avidly sought by ship crews from across the world.

Directly west of San Jose del Cabo, Palmilla Point extends a small arm of protection against the efforts of the pulsing surf. And in the apex of this more quiet cove, Palmilla Hotel tethers its little fleet of sport fishing boats. The hotel structure perches importantly above, on a black rock eminence; its great sheets of window glass peer from under sweeping shadowed eaves, like weather eyes, looking out to sea.

Palmilla and the next two Cape hotels in line, Cabo San Lucas and the Hacienda, all have their own airstrips carved to windward in the raw, red land. The hotels are imposing structures, the more striking because of their wilderness settings. Cabo San Lucas Hotel, with its gleaming white walls and red-tiled roofs, might very well have been plucked from a Mediterranean shore. Elegant statuary points up a series of pools and terraces that descend gently to a ribbon of beach at water's edge.

In early afternoon the fleets of little charter boats come speeding in, as if suddenly magnetized out of nowhere, to their respective coves—like white chargers flying aloft their battle pennants. Marlin and sailfish are transported ashore, and for a while all is activity about the resort. Later, music drifts from shaded verandas. It's cocktail time, and sunburned, happy fishermen talk of the day's catch. Shadows lengthen. Mares'-tails in the sky change from cotton-white to rose and crimson, and the huge, gold globe of sun is sucked beneath a darkening sea. Night comes quickly below the Tropic of Cancer.

The most recently built hotel in the area is the Hacienda on the beach at Cape San Lucas, only a few sandy steps from the Cape's older business enterprise, its fish cannery. The village proper is set back a mile inland from the beach, the better to weather severe southerlies (chubascos) that strike with little warning in late September and early October. This community is not large, and only a minimum of supplies are available, with the

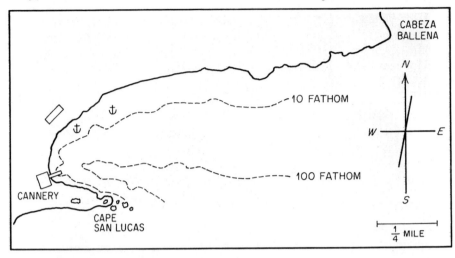

CAPE SAN LUCAS
22 deg. 53 m. North lat.
109 deg. 54 m. W. Long.

Approach to San Lucas Bay should be made in daylight because there is no light on Cape San Lucas, which forms the southeastern extremity of the Bay, nor can the light on the cannery dock be depended upon. There is deep water within 400 yards of the shoreline from Cape Falso to Cape San Lucas, and within San Lucas Bay, the 50-fathom curve is within ¼ mile of the beach. When approaching from the northwest, round Cape San Lucas and take a heading of approximately 315 deg. magnetic toward the prominent hotel. There is a shelf with approximately 5 to 8 fathoms of water, hard sand bottom, that should be located; care should be taken to be well over the shelf to avoid having the anchor drag off into water that deepens rapidly to 50 fathoms or more. When taking on fuel or water from the cannery dock, it is common practice to drop an anchor close by the dock, and back to the dock until a short stern line can be used to hold the stern toward it. This is done because of a moderate swell which runs in the Bay. The beach at the northwest side of the dock affords relatively easy landing under most weather conditions. During the summer months of mid-August to mid-October the Bay is frequently unsafe, because no protection is afforded from easterly and southerly winds, which often reach gale force.

exception of fine fresh produce for sale at a nearby Japanese-operated farm. Once again, the availability of water for irrigation turns otherwise arid soil to one of astounding productivity.

Beyond the massive gray monoliths, "The Friars," the most impressive sight here at the Cape is found on the ocean side of the point, where prevailing winds and currents sweep the sea into giant breakers and carve weird sculptures in ancient sand-

"The Friars," last rocky monoliths marking the most southerly end of the Baja Peninsula, at Cabo San Lucas.

stone cliffs. A narrow valley lies secluded above a line of sandy dunes. Shielded from scouring winds, wild flowers form a carpet beneath towering wild fig trees. Boulders, house-size and larger, are scattered at intervals amidst the native shrubbery, offering little caves of weather sanctuary.

In 1948 when I first visited this private hideaway, I thought, "Here's where I would like to retire." Three years later when I looked in again, I found an old man living there. He was cooking a savory stew of fish and rice over a small campfire. On a subsequent trip to the Cape, some four years later, "my" retirement plot was occupied by a group of guitar-playing, bearded fellows with very dirty feet. I guess I didn't want to retire, anyway!

CHAPTER 5

Cape San Lucas to Cedros Island

Ever since its discovery by one of Cortez' skippers in 1537, Cape San Lucas has been a refuge cove and a watering place for boats from all points of the globe. These aspects have changed but little through the centuries; only the boats themselves have been modernized. All else is pretty much the same, except that perhaps there are not so many pirates nowadays. (Or maybe the same number, but better camouflaged.) In any event, "I'll meet you at the Cape" is a common phrase for those heading up or down coast. And after many days at sea, there is always the welcome feeling of mingling again with those who have had familiar experiences in their recent watery wanderings.

During the season, there are often no less than a dozen pleasure craft at anchor, for varying spans of time, at Cape San Lucas Cove. The anchorage marks a sort of dividing line. For those heading northwest up-coast, crews are busy fueling and watering, bringing warm jackets and foul-weather gear up from below-decks. Many of these boat owners fly home from this port (if they have not already flown out of La Paz) leaving a crew to bring the boat back the long, uphill haul to the States. For the sailor headed around to the Gulf, or across to Mazatlan and south along the Mexican mainland coast, he too is concerned with reorganization, readying his boat for warmer climes. He may be mending sails, replacing broken "bats," or scouring salt from himself and his craft. Whatever new heading is to be taken, a rendezvous at the Cape, with its interval of friendly camaraderie, adds a pleasant and memorable interlude for all who sail near its port.

Of our own six trips up the Pacific from Mexico, four were rough trips and two were reasonably smooth. No one can foretell precisely what the weather will bring. Time of year means a lot, however, in such forecasting. Our four rough trips were in January or February. Of the two smoother cruises one took place in

Newest of Cape resort hotels is Hacienda Cabo San Lucas, shown here in picture center. Cannery dock where fuel and pure spring water are available is to left (not shown), hidden behind foreground rock. Best anchorage at Cape San Lucas is in the area just offshore the Hacienda Hotel.

March, and the other in late May. From this and from others' experiences, a possible weather guide may be drawn.

Mexican fishing-boat operators can be depended upon for their wise judgment concerning weather forecasting and suggested anchorage protection—logically enough, as most of their lives are spent afloat in the area. Their lives and cargoes depend upon their proper assay of both fish and weather habits. Most of them speak only Spanish, but usually there will be someone on the "party line" (marine radio frequencies 2182, 2638 or 2738 kc's) who can translate if necessary. The usual procedure before take-off at San Lucas is to visit the cannery office for recent weather reports from the fishing fleet operating from that base. And it should go without saying that when the big purse-seiners come steaming into the Cape harbor minus full holds of fish, this is a good indication that the winds outside are strong and seas lumpy.

If this sounds too precautionary, it is not meant to intimidate, but only to point out that from the Cape by direct line to the next harbor of refuge to the northwest, there is a span of about 165 miles. For those with fuel limitations, a radius-of-action problem might have to be taken into consideration, should one decide to return to the Cape because of inclement weather or mechanical difficulties.

There are only a few small and only partially sheltered anchorages along this leg: namely, south of San Pedro Point, where there is a small village (but rough-surf shore access), and below Marquis Point. Local fishing boats anchor in these small bites, on occasion, but they are not recommended for anyone without local knowledge. Normally one takes a heading of 290 degrees from abeam Cabo Falso and makes a direct run to Redondo Point, the southerly entrance to Magdalena Bay. If head winds are too strong for comfort on this heading, some protection is usually gained by following the shoreline contour along the 10-fathom depth line.

On the seaward side of Cabo San Lucas, sandstone is sculptured into weird forms. Sea birds nest in some of the stone's apertures.

On one of our recent cruises running northwest from the Cape, we experienced another of our many reasons to bless our radar unit. It was shortly after midnight. Gordon and I were on watch, and our position was about 50 miles northwest of Cabo Falso. The night was clear with stars, but no moon. The vista ahead (even on the radarscope at first) was completely black. Every half-hour or so, I changed the range down to the 10-mile, 4- and then 1-mile scale, for a closer inspection of any possible traffic near us. On one such range-switch, I suddenly saw a group of small targets ahead of us, about 5 miles distant. We put the grid on them to plot their course, if any.

"That's odd," I remarked, "whatever the targets are, they're not moving. We're closing in on them only at the rate of our own speed." (About 10½ knots.)

Gordon took the binoculars out on the foredeck, to try to visually pick out some lights or other indication of what the blips might be, but nothing was visible except dark sky and blacker water. From the size of the blips, which were now positioned at only 1 mile ahead, we knew we could visually see navigational lights if there were any there.

"Maybe they're sea-monsters, Mom," Gordon joked. "Let's turn on the searchlight. Maybe it will give us a clue."

The moment our light focused ahead, voilà, seven fishing boats burst into bloom—running lights, masthead lights and stern lights. It looked like a group of lighted Christmas trees bobbing on the swells. So these were our mysterious radar targets—Mexican fishing boats, floating dead in the water, probably saving their current by dousing all lights.

As we altered course to avoid them, we both wondered aloud if our searchlight aroused their crews to display their position, or if we would have made big boats into little pieces had we not detected their presence on radar. As the natives say, "Quien sabe?" —Who knows?

Although charts (and uncorrected data in *H.O. Sailing Directions*) list a possible anchorage northeast of Point Tasco at the southern end of Isla Santa Margarita, this is no longer the case. Shoaling has increased so that it is no longer a safe anchorage. Magdalena Bay, with its entrance at the northwest end of the Island, is the target for boats seeking shelter and/or fuel before continuing northwest along the Peninsula.

There are several choices of good anchorages in Magdalena Bay (see chartlet). Our favorite has always been Man of War Cove,

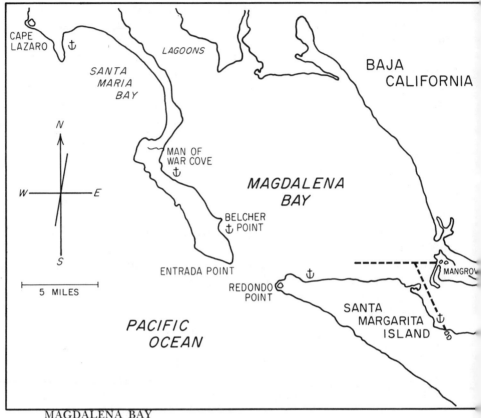

MAGDALENA BAY
24 deg. 35 min. N. Lat.
112 deg. 00 min. W. Long.

Once inside Magdalena Bay, anchorage can be taken at many places along the northern side of Santa Margarita Island, or along the tongue of peninsula extending from Man of War Cove to Entrada Point. Within ¼ mile of the light at Man of War Cove there is from 5 to 10 fathoms of water, and from 3 to 5 fathoms within 1000 feet of the beach. North and northeast of this anchorage there are extensive shoals, which should be approached only with a small boat or tender. Good anchorage is also available just under Belcher Point, although the sounder should be used when approaching it because it is relatively shallow. If Puerto Cortes (where fuel and limited supplies of water may be obtained) is the destination, the ranges on Mangrove Island and on Margarita Island must be used to avoid the shallow waters on either side of the ranged channels. The Mexican Navy maintains a dock and airstrip at Puerto Cortes, and a cannery is also located here. During the occasional strong northeast blows during the summer months, none of the anchorages named are comfortable and Santa Maria Bay will provide better protection.

lying to port about 8 miles beyond the Bay entrance.

This is a very small community of fishermen and their families, for many years presided over by the late Port Captain Senor Gregorio Vidal. He was a friend of countless yachtsmen from the States, and his son continues the tradition set by his father.

Some ten miles to the north of Man of War Cove, reached through a rather tricky but buoyed channel, is the new commercial port of San Carlos. A good road connects it with La Paz on the opposite side of the Peninsula and the rich farmland region between. Coastal freighters now carry much of the produce from lower Baja California to Ensenada, and cargoes southbound, without the need to round the Cape to pick up or deliver freight at the docks of La Paz. Nearly 300 miles of sea travel are saved with the development of this commercial facility.

The Navy and cannery anchorages, across the Bay to the southeast, will usually have limited amounts of fuel and water, but one should not expect to find foodstores available at any of Magdalena Bay communities (other than their bountiful supply of fish, which are yours for the catching).

When time was available, we have always enjoyed a day or two of gunk-holing by dinghy from Man of War Cove, into the mangrove-lined lagoons that wind for several miles into the northern reaches of the Bay. Protected by sun-warmed rolling hills and sand dunes that divide the Pacific from the Bay, such a junket provides a rest, and pleasant contrast from the ocean's energetic bounce and blow.

On one of these occasions, we loaded our tender to its gunwales with picnic lunches, bags for shell-gathering, fishing gear, snorkels and fins, ad infinitum. It was going to be an all-day exploration. However, having forgotten to take along our outboard-motor repair kit, it almost turned out to be a "forever" trip! While returning from the lagoon to its point of entry into the Bay, the motor stopped. Nothing could induce it to start. There was no choice but to row. Once away from the estuary, we felt the full force of a strong off-shore wind blowing against us, pushing us away from the western shoreline. Also, the tide was going out. Even with two strong men rowing, the combination of wind and tide was drifting us further into the middle of the 17-mile-wide Bay.

One of our group tried to rig a sail using a large beach towel, but the elements held their advantage. Fortunately, the receding tide finally took us over a shoaling sand bar where the water was only hip-deep. Two of us jumped out to guide and push the dinghy toward shore, leaving one couple aboard to continue bending their backs at the oars. Then one oar broke; more pushing, and wind still howling. But we were at least making some progress toward safety. Every so often, a small sting ray would dart to the surface near our legs, but this seemed a minor danger compared with the possibility of having ourselves and dinghy carried away from shore. After an hour's exertion, we had the small boat a few yards from the beach. I swam ashore and offered to haul the boat by its bow line back to Man of War Cove. "Oh, no," said the men, "we're safe now. We can paddle and sail along here in the shore protection." Not me! I walked back, on good old terra firma.

Inspecting giant clam shells, found along lagoon shores which wind for miles inland from Man of War Cove at Magdalena Bay.

For those taking their boats to Puerto Cortes, in southwestern Magdalena Bay, the safest procedure is to run this dogleg course slowly and with careful attention to the ranges which point up the devious channel. The first of these markers lines up with the northern end of Mangrove Island; then after an approximate 64-degree turn to starboard, align with another pair of ranges (lighted at night) which are situated on a hill beyond the Port. This course is well defined on Bahia Magdalena Detailed Chart #1636.

During spring months, whether entering or leaving Magdalena Bay, one is often accompanied on all sides by whales—and it is not a rare sight to see one of these huge grays leaping clear of the ocean, with a quick writhing and twisting motion. It is said that this is a way the whale rids himself of annoying ramoras that attach themselves to his hide.

Moving on northwest out of the Bay, another good anchorage may be found in the northern arm of Santa Maria Bay, where 868-foot Smart Peak and 1300-foot San Lazaro Peak, forming Hughes Point, shield the cove from prevailing northwest winds. This is a huge empty bay, with white sand beaches curving its indentation to meet a constantly booming surf. Were it not for its isolation, Santa Maria Bay would be a surfer's heaven, with its 15-mile arc of giant breakers and nothing but gulls and sandpipers ashore.

Out of the anchorage behind Hughes Point weather conditions usually determine a course on up the coast. With mild winds and seas, most sailors take a direct heading for Turtle Bay or for Cedros Island. During winter months, however, there are apt to be northeasterly winds of varying intensity, making the going slower and inviting refuge coves more often. In such cases, one may prefer hugging the 10-fathom line offshore to seek partial protection at Pequena Bay, Ballenas, San Hipolito, Asuncion, San Roque and San Pablo Bays.

On our first cruise up-coast in this particular area we had our only occasion to find it advisable to turn and run to sea. It was early January, and a northeast gale had made up in the matter of hours. With family and friends aboard *Monsoon I,* our 104-foot, triple-screw ship, we were on a direct heading from Cape Lazaro to Ballenas Bay—a target we never reached.

Ever since leaving the Cape weather had been rough, and was now worsening. I had been making innumerable trips to the engine room, to throttle back and throttle back again, from our

Monsoon II bites into a big one, while running up the coast northwest of Cabo San Lucas.

cruise speed of 12 knots finally down to 6. As night wore on, winds increased to 40 and 50 knots, with higher gusts. Our poor, belabored ship would spring off one huge roller and drop with a resounding thud into yet another trough.

"This is just getting too hard on her," Jack finally said. "We'll take her out to sea till the gale blows through." I timed our course change in the log and went below again for bridge orders. With throttle full-ahead on the starboard engine and down to slow on the port, and with a series of sickening lurches, we pivoted around 120 degrees to a southwest heading—down wind. Although this was a less arduous course, it took extra strength for the helmsman to keep the ship from yawing overly. We spelled each other at half-hour intervals at the wheel.

My mother was with us on this trip (her first sea-voyage, and one she thought would be her last!). Mom is not a sailor, despite the fact that Nathaniel Bowditch was one of her *great* great-granduncles. I was concerned that she might become dehydrated, as she had been seasick ever since we had left the Cape. For the last eight hours it had been too rough to cook. Those in their bunks weren't hungry, and the four of us on watch had each fended for himself from the galley. However, I decided I would make some hot biscuits and brew a pot of tea for Mother, on the chance she would be able to retain some nourishment.

It was a real feat to prepare the food and at the same time to stay upright in our dancing galley. Finally I had my chore finished, and felt proud of the accomplishment. I carried the meal in to Mother's stateroom in a small basket—a tray would have been useless. Then it was my turn at the wheel again, after which, another trip to the engine room to top off lube oil in our three diesels. Eventually I was able to get back to Mother's stateroom, to see how she was faring.

"Did you like your supper, Mom?" I asked expectantly.

"The tea was very nice," Mother answered, "but next time, Carolyn, I wish you would try to get more *salt* in your biscuits." (I guess my resulting laughter bordered on hysteria.)

After nine hours of running before the seas, the winds had somewhat abated and we turned back on a course for Asuncion. By first light of the second day, land loomed ahead through our sea-smeared windows. Bone-weary, we dropped anchor in Asuncion Bay. Our bunks had never before felt so soft and inviting!

Asuncion, like Turtle Bay and Cedros Island village to the northwest, are all fish cannery settlements where a variety of products are processed. One of their richest harvests of the sea is abalone, some of which is canned and another portion frozen for export markets. The life of the abalone-diver is a strenuous one. He arises at dawn and works an approximate six-hour day, six days a week; diving often to a depth of 150 feet. During abalone season, mid-March through October, the divers risk moray eels, swift underwater currents and pressure dangers, to bring up an average of 200 abalone per hour. Some of the divers wear Scuba gear, and others full diving dress with air lines from the decks of their helpers' small boats.

"It's a good life," one young native told us. "We make up to $40 per day while we're diving, and our helpers who handle our air hoses and clean the ab's get $20 a day. Besides, we *like* diving!" The boy went on to explain that the most obvious danger

A noisy seal family bark at our approach, Asuncion Harbor.

of the deep, the shark, has never bothered them. Perhaps the sharks are so well-fed with other fish in these warm, productive waters, they cannot be concerned with this new predator descending with his bubbling airhose, his prying-irons and baskets.

Turtle Bay, despite its safe anchorage and economic affluence, is not a picture postcard spa. All fresh water must be brought by boat, 20 miles across the ocean from Cedros Island, or during canning season, distilled from sea water in the processing boiler. Rainfall is practically unheard of in the area. With neither tree nor shrub nor blade of grass to relieve the vista of sear tans and browns, Turtle Bay's little huddle of dusty dwellings appears to have taken on the protective coloring of its environment, as if by lying there couchant, immobile and feigning death, it might somehow escape extinction from the scouring wind and sun.

Its hospitable inhabitants, however, are lively with good spirits. "We have no water to spare," they will say, "but would you like some fresh hot bread or rolls? Some lobsters, perhaps? Maybe a few cans of abalone? We have much of that."

Less tangible, yet most important, the natives of Turtle Bay have contentment—very much of that. Certainly no foreign element eyes with greed their tiny hamlet. The only war they know is with the elements—the wind, the sun, the sea.

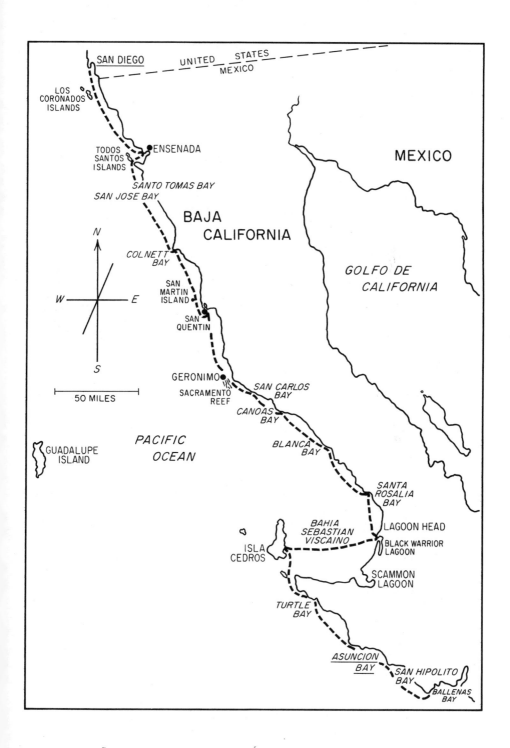

CHAPTER 6

Cedros Island to San Diego

Twelve miles south of Cedros Island, Point Eugenio marks the southern spur of the great bay of Sebastian Viscaino. Although the word "bay" is ordinarily considered an area of protected water, here such is not the case. All during cruising season, November to June, one may expect northerly winds in this region of anywhere from 10 to 40 knots. Sometimes these blows decrease with sunset but just as often they continue in intensity for days and nights at a time. For this reason the several lee anchorages on the eastern side of Cedros Island are oft-sought refuge coves by both pleasure boats and the fishing fleet.

Dewey Channel, separating Point Eugenio and Natividad Island, is the favored course in approaching Cedros from the south. In negotiating this 4-mile wide channel, one should stay well to the eastern side to clear rocks and shoals surrounding the southeastern end of Natividad. When abeam Point Eugenio, a course of 330 degrees puts one on a direct heading for Cedros Village, the Island's only permanent settlement.

Early-day sailors were first attracted to the Island because of the availability of pure spring water as well as the advantages of shelter. From the 16th century, sailing ships paused at Cedros' southeast shores to fill their water casks at the spring and lighter them out to their vessels. Today there is a short length of hose from the Village's cannery dock to fill small-boat water tanks *if* surge will permit. For deeper draft boats, the lightering process is still necessary for taking on water or any other ship supplies. Shore going is accomplished by taking a tender to the dock, securing it to pilings and then climbing a vertical ladder to the top of the dock.

The fish cannery at Cedros Village is its chief economy. Beyond its plant and warehouses, a small group of homes climbs up a red slant of earth. At the top of the first rise is the church with

Looking down on the anchorage below Cedros Village, Cedros Island.

its twin belfry towers. The school and a few more tiny homes are sprinkled at intervals on higher reaches of the slope. Just to the north looms the nearly 4000-foot peak of Mt. Cedros, alternately displaying or hiding its green-forested dome in a blue-black mass of cumulo-nimbus. Rain is not infrequent on the island, and this, combined with several mountain springs, makes livelihood possible for deer, goats and other wildlife.

On a recent visit to Cedros Village, we were amazed to see a half-dozen television antennae sprouting from some of the roof-tops. One of our friends invited us into his home to see his TV and proudly turned the set on to show us the snowy outline of an old movie originating in San Diego, over 300 miles and several intervening mountains distant. A freak in television transmission provides this isolated community with a fairly regular series of pictures and sound, much to the delight of the inhabitants.

Another diversion for the Cedros Island people, which surprised us, was the sight of a small fleet of automobiles thundering around the few miles of road the Island possesses. Why anyone would want or find need of a car at this remote island remains a conjecture. Everything in the Village lies but a few steps up or downhill. The road certainly appears to be a road to nowhere, and the car owners must have been more than reasonably affluent to afford the cost of their cars' transportation from the mainland by freighter to the Island.

East of Cedros Island, Scammon's Lagoon reaches back into the Peninsula nearly forty miles. This many-armed shallow bay is notable as the West Coast's greatest whale-calving nursery. Each fall the great gray whales move south 6000 miles from their summer home in Alaska's Bering Sea to produce their young in the warm quiet waters of Scammon's Lagoon. Once threatened with extinction from early-day whalers, the grays have since 1937 been protected by the International Whaling Agreement. Now their count has risen to an estimated 6 or 7000 head. On one recent November week, 1,421 whales were counted passing at the whale-counting station in LaJolla, California, attesting to the fact their numbers are increasing.

Although on a few occasions medium-sized boats have negotiated these shoaling Lagoon waters, such ventures were only possible with aircraft lending guidance to passable waters. Such was the system used a few years ago when Dr. Paul Dudley White's party of scientists inched their boats into the Lagoon to study the heartbeat of the whale, a research program that had as an objective human-heart knowledge and repair. Without this aid from airplane or helicopter for guidance, the finest navigator would have difficulty in even locating the Lagoon's entrance, much less in negotiating its shifting sandbars.

Not all of the gray whales calve inside the confines of Scammon's Lagoon; occasionally a birth occurs in the ocean. It was a rare sight, one December day, to see a great circle of porpoises swimming near the surface. In the center of their protective ring was a gray whale, about to give birth. Obviously the porpoises, mammals of the whale species, were guarding the laboring whale from any dangerous marauders—sharks, barracuda or humans. After the whale calf was born and safely protected by its mother, the porpoises bowed out of their self-imposed guard, broke ranks and sped away.

Approximately 15 miles north of Scammon's Lagoon is a similar but more populated indentation into the peninsula's desert region, Black Warrior (Guerrero Negro) Lagoon, site of a 250,000-acre salt-mining operation. Unlike Scammon's, Black Warrior's 7-mile entrance channel is kept dredged to a depth of 32 feet, permitting commercial vessel traffic. The first of this 99.4%-pure sodium chloride was taken from Black Warrior's port in 1880. Then in 1951 the nucleus of the Ocean Salt Company was launched, and by 1962 as many as a hundred ships were calling at the port to bring out yearly over a million tons of salt. A large part of the raw product is used in the southland in chemical and other industries. Its major markets, however, are approximately 700,000 tons sent each year to Japan, some 400,000 tons to the Pacific northwest and other smaller shipments to Europe. Present prospects point toward this Mexican salt distillery becoming the world's largest in output.

Black Warrior's port town, Venustiano Carranza, is extremely modern in appearance; its streets paved with gypsum, a chlorinated water system, sewers and well-constructed public buildings. Its airport is abuzz with small airplanes coming and going on their errands connected with the salt mine. Since there is less than 2 inches of rain per year, a minimum of humidity and temperature rarely over 80 degrees, the climate is ideal for salt distillation. Sixty-ton salt loaders are built like grain harvesters and can load a truck in seven minutes. Glistening like huge snowbanks, the conical hills of salt awaiting export at Black Warrior can be seen from as far as 10 miles at sea.

It was in this area that one of our friends, Milt Farney, was harbor-hopping a few years ago in the *Searcher,* a boat incredibly small for these waters—an 18-foot outboard! He had called at Black Warrior for gasoline and supplies and was on his way out the channel when a call came over his radiophone from another boat. "We are low on fresh water," the other skipper advised. "Can any boat in this vicinity spare us some?" Milt checked his own meager water container, then replied, "Yes, I guess I could let you have about three quarts. I've a pretty good beer supply." There was a moment of (probably stunned) silence on the airwaves before the other voice came back: "That will hardly be enough." A short chuckle. "We are the — [a freighter]; we need at least a couple hundred gallons."

A half-hour later, Milt's tiny outboard met the approaching freighter coming into harbor. Now that the respective skippers were alerted to each other's identity there were deep-throated hoots of recognition from the ship and responding tinny blasts from Milt's hand-horn. When abeam, the freighter's Captain came out on his bridge and called down to Milt, "Well, thanks anyway, *Searcher,* for your offer. You're sure you don't want something from US?"

Heading on northwesterly along the upper contours of Bahia Sebastian Viscaino there are a fair number of small anchorages

affording varying degrees of protection from prevailing winds—
Lagoon Head, Santa Rosalia Bay, Blanca, Canoas and San Carlos
Bays. They are adequately described in H.O. #84, but none have
shore access nor facilities. From a safety standpoint, the span
from Canoas Point to Point Antonio should be covered during
daylight hours to avoid the dangerous shoals in the 2¼-mile-long
expanse of Sacramento Reef. At low tide and with reasonably
calm seas, breaking water is plainly visible across the more prominent pinnacles of this vicious reef. Well-known but uncharted in
1872, this reef gained its name when the 271-foot side-wheel
steamer *Sacramento* foundered on its rocky shoals while coming
up the coast from Panama. Within minutes after striking the reef
the ship filled with water to its freight deck. Its eighty passengers
and crew were fortunate in making their escape to nearby Geronimo Island and five days later they were rescued by the
steamer *Montana*. The *Sacramento's* 268 tons of merchandise
cargo and $1,500,000 of coins, bound for San Francisco from
Mazatlan, was salvaged, but remains of the ship's hull still attract
adventurous skin-divers who frequent the waters around Sacramento Reef.

There is a ten-second white flashing light, visible from about
13 miles distant, on Geronimo Island some 10 miles north of
Sacramento Reef. Fair anchorage may be found on the island's
easterly side, though a cautious approach is indicated due to
outcropping rocks and kelp.

Guadalupe Island, lying 140 miles west and slightly south of
Geronimo, is perhaps best known to fishermen and scientific survey parties. Until recently it was ruled off-limits to yachtsmen
because of certain archaeological studies then being conducted
ashore. Best anchorage is at the southeastern end of the Island
where the Mexican Government maintains a weather and radio
station. Manned by some 20 Navy personnel, they were most
cordial to us during a recent Christmas-time visit.

San Quentin (San Kin-teen) and Hassler's Cove, the latter protected by San Martin Island, are the two favored anchorages
along this portion of the coastline. San Quentin is perhaps the
most often sought of the two by pleasure boats cruising up or
down the coast. It was once a seaport for the shipment of grain
and other products grown or mined in the vicinity. But as is historical throughout Baja, the foreign interests (in this case British) found their business methods incompatible with those of
the natives, and both mine and milling ventures dwindled to

extinction. Now San Quentin is almost a ghost town except for the recent advent of several guest ranches situated in the nearby coastal valley and available for touring hunters and fishermen. Two airstrips serve private or charter-plane pilots while hardier travelers drive the 240 miles of partially paved highway down from San Diego.

Pismo clams, lobster and abalone abound along San Quentin's bayshore, beside the ever-present ocean fish. Ducks, geese and black sea-brandt frequent the coastal area from October until April. And for the minority group (those of us who hunt only with camera, or with hands for the inert stone, the shell, or piece of twisted driftwood) the Bay also presents a wealth of beach-combings where tides roll in regularly to deposit their flotsam: glass net-floats from Japan, fragile sea-fans from some south-sea shore, gnarled fists of hardwood polished to a high red lustre— all are flung along the strand with their less exotic driftmates, the bottle, the carton, the can. This polyglot tide of trinkets appear, for some geophysical quirk, to become pocketed here at San Quentin's nearly landlocked harbor as nowhere else along Baja's ocean coast. Even for the non-collector it's an unusual show; "pop" art of the sea.

Without local knowledge and without shallow draft, boats should not be taken across the treacherous bar from San Quentin Bay to the inner (former) harbor. Best anchorage area is in the northeast part of the Bay, although there are plans now under development for a protected small-boat harbor and marina facilities which may replace the ghost-town face of this historic bayfront. Already dredging operations are in progress with the spoils taken upcoast to Todos Santos Bay and used there as land-fill for a new seaside resort at Ensenada.

Roughly 12 miles northwest of San Quentin is San Martin Island, a nearly 500-foot high extinct volcano. The Island has recently added a navigational light and has two good anchorages. The best in prevailing northwesterlies is Hassler's Cove, on the east side; the other is on the southeast shore in the lee of a low neck of rocky outcroppings. (See chart.) Due to the topography of adjacent peninsula shores where mountain peaks rear abruptly from sea level to 4 to 5000 feet and to extreme temperature variations between inland desert heat and cool ocean waters, winds along this particular section are apt to be erratic. Sometimes they will switch 180 degrees in as many seconds. One may be snugly anchored one moment, and dragging all over the cove

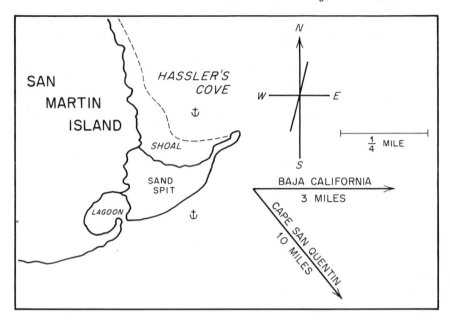

SAN MARTIN ISLAND
30 deg. 29 min. N. lat.
116 deg. 07 min. W. long.

There are 10 fathoms of water within ½ mile of the Baja California Peninsula to the east, and within ⅛ mile of the east side of San Martin Island, and there are no outlying obstructions along either shore. The conically shaped island has an extinct volcanic crater nearly in its center. Extending north-eastward is a low sand spit with what appears to be a stone breakwater at its extremity. Anchorage is most generally taken in Hassler Cove, which affords moderate protection from prevailing winds and seas. During heavy winds from the northwest, anchorage on the south side of the sand spit affords better protection. Some kelp extends from the lagoon along the sand spit, which should be avoided when anchoring. Landing on either side of the sand spit can usually be done with the average dinghy, during the early part of the day and before normal afternoon winds commence blowing.

the next. We have often experienced such abrupt wind changes, particularly at Colnett Bay, some 32 miles northwest of San Martin. Here the winds will freakishly switch to slam in on an anchored boat from the east or south, even though its direction is still strong from the northwest outside this circular harbor.

There are two more coves of partial refuge up-coast from Cape Colnett before reaching Baja's last Pacific port of call at Ensenada. These are found at San Jose and Santo Tomas Bay. To be sure, the former is heavily ridden with kelp, and the latter anchorage proves an obstacle course for boats moving into its small protection. (Santo Tomas Bay is an export station for lobster, and traps used for holding them for shipment are scattered at random across the harbor.) But despite the many lacks in these and other peninsula coastal refuge coves, when sanctuary is needed, any of them will appear heaven-sent to the weary skipper and his crew.

Ten miles westward across the Bay from Ensenada, the Todos Santos Islands offer another small sheltered bight on their eastern shores for a rest or refuge anchorage. Uninhabited except for itinerant native fishing camps, the Islands have easy access to shore and their water-carved caves and arches are interesting to explore by dinghy. Dive if you will for lobster and abalone which line the rocky island shoreline, but remember that under Mexican law, none of this shellfish may be taken across the U.S. border.

Ensenada is not typical of other Mexican communities to the south; a border town never is. But it does have its own charm and appeal, especially so during its several annual fiestas. The week-before-Christmas celebration of La Posada and the week-long Mardi Gras carnival preceding Lent are two of the most

Mardi Gras parade and fiesta held annually at Ensenada.

festive celebrations, with daily parades, dancing and, always, the inimitable native music.

Each year this port plays host and finish line for the colossus of all sailing races, the Cinco de Mayo (May fifth) contest which starts at Newport, California and has for the last several years included well over 400 sailing entrants. Ensenada's ample harbor offers good anchorage within its breakwaters, but as afternoon northwest winds are generally a brisk 15 to 20 knots, the wise skipper will be certain to pay out sufficient anchor chain before leaving his boat unattended. There are no slips available for visiting boats, but native water-taxi service is inexpensive. Or the visitor's own dinghy can be used and tied to floats used by the water-taxis.

Ensenada's history since the 1880's has been a colorful series of contrasts: once a gold-rush center and a crossroads for soldiers of fortune from Europe and the Orient, it thrived with a winery, a tannery, a soap factory and flour mill. In 1887 it became Mexico's territorial capital, with its prosperity heightened by a British firm leasing 16 million acres of farmland from the Mexican government and investing huge sums in roads, a wharf and a spur railroad. By the early 1900's however, the gold veins were depleted. The English Company, as the syndicate was known, failed in its grandiose undertakings and moved away. Ensenada dwindled to nothing—a ravished ghost town—and the capital site was moved inland to Mexicali. For the next twenty years the small remaining populace subsisted primarily by fishing.

Tourism commenced Ensenada's upswing toward prosperity when, in 1930, ex-boxing champion Jack Dempsey financed the construction of a lavish gambling casino, Hotel Playa, later known as El Riviera del Pacifico. Although gambling was declared illegal in Mexico only two short years after the Casino's opening, this was enough to start an ever-increasing tide of tourists to Ensenada. In 1958 a Mexican harbor improvement program was responsible for the completion of a 54-million peso breakwater protecting what had been strictly open roadstead. This, coupled with an upgrading of roads and irrigation in the fertile inland farmlands, has combined to strengthen the economy of Baja's largest ocean port where cotton export rates highest of its varied products.

Commercial ships and pleasure boats from all over the world may be seen at any time in Ensenada's duty-free port. And elsewhere in town and along the sunny beachfront there are many

Looking down from Chapultepec Hill on Ensenada and harbor.

new hotels, restaurants and gift shops. Charter sport-fishing boats move in and out of harbor, trailed by a wake of gulls. High on Chapultepec Hill overlooking Todos Santos Bay, real estate subdividers are hard at work building more miles of residential streets and erecting scores of modern homes—vari-colored houses which rise as formal rows of flowers against this balding sun-baked hill.

So grows the long-touted "forgotten land" of Baja California. One by one the tiny village assumes first the outline of a city, then of a budding spa. Tourist and new-business seeker alike march into line, as an ant colony moving steadily into that long, strange finger of land we know as Lower California. Each is drawn to his own "discovery": the fish, the salubrious climate, the palm-shaded but short-lived hideaway.

Meanwhile the high-humped mountain spine bisecting Baja's longitude broods over its hidden wealth of precious stones and minerals, once briefly sought and fought for. Along with tourist dollars now flowing in with pleasure boating, mining may yet provide Baja with its biggest boom.

The 60-mile run from Ensenada to the border and San Diego may be run fairly close to shore, the better to note the coast's significant signs of economic growth. Only a decade ago these shores were as devoid of habitation as is much of the peninsula's lower region. Now clusters of motels, shopping centers and beach resorts appear to spring up overnight, insidiously merging to form a nearly unbroken line of facilities for passing motorists along the coastal highway extending from the U.S. to Tijuana and Ensenada.

In clear weather and when abeam Descanso Point, four rock islands called Los Coronados rise above the horizon ahead, and are normally passed to port. Waters around their barren perimeters are favorite fishing grounds in this ocean segment, but due to a lack of shore access, nothing but seals and birds live on the islands proper, except for the lighthouse keepers on South Coronado Island.

Ten miles beyond the Coronados sway the long line of red and black buoys marking San Diego's entrance channel, and boats from Mexican waters slow to a halt at the well-marked Harbor Master's dock on Shelter Island for Customs Clearance into the United States.

Appendix to Part I

Facilities and Supplies
Books and Charts
Resort Hotels for Information and Reservations
Mexican Requirements for Clearance of Pleasure Boats
Electric/Electronic Equipment
Spare Parts—Engine or Sail
Imports—Merchandise, Liquor
Air and Ferry Transportation to Baja Calif.
Fishing Calendar—Upper Gulf, Loreto and Vicinity, Cape area,
    Coast and Gulf
Marine Weather Reports
Fueling and Watering
Fenders
Mechanical and Hull repairs
Types of Boat suitable for Baja California Cruising
Table of Distances between Harbors and Anchorages

FOOD SUPPLIES FOR MEXICAN CRUISING

Fish—there is no dearth of sea or shell fish around the Baja Peninsula. For the non-fisherman, whatever fish are in season may be purchased from natives or even presented by overstocked compatriots.

Fresh Meat—Resort restaurants ordinarily have much of their food stuffs, including meats, flown in from Mexico City. Its quality is comparable to that in this country. Locally raised beef and pork (only occasionally available) is not aged. Some sailors carry a meat grinder aboard to render this unhung meat chewable. More often, canned or frozen U.S. meats are carried aboard.

FACILITIES AND SUPPLIES—PENINSULA OF BAJA CALIFORNIA

San Felipe	A			G **	H		R	S		W **
Kino Bay				G **	H			S		W **
Guaymas	A	B	D	G	H	M	R	S	T	W
Bahia de Los Angeles	A			G **	H			S *		W **
Santa Rosalia	A		D *	G **				S	T	
Mulege	A			G **	H		R	S		W **
Loreto	A			G **	H		R	S		W **
La Paz	A	B	D	G	H	M	R	S	T	W
Las Cruces	A				H		R			
Las Palmas	A			G **	H		R			W **
Buena Vista	A			G **	H		R			W **
Palmilla Hotel	A				H		R			
Hotel Cabo San Lucas	A				H		R			
Hacienda Cabo S. Lucas	A				H		R			
Cabo San Lucas (village)	A		D	G	H		R	S	T	W
Puerto Cortes (Magdalena Bay)			D *	G *						W *
Ascuncion				G **				S *		W **
Turtle Bay			D *	G **				S *		
Cedros Island (village)			D	G *				S	T	W
Black Warrior			D *	G *				S *	T	W *
Ensenada	A	B	D	G	H	M	R	S	T	W

Key

A—air service, scheduled or charter
B—butane gas
D—diesel fuel
G—gasoline
H--hotel(s)
M—mechanical repairs

R—restaurant
S—supplies
T—telegraph office
W—water
*—limited amounts
**—limited and lightered

Mexican homemade bread may almost always be purchased at any community where a half-dozen or more families make their homes. And this is delicious "pan" (bread, pronounced "pon") by anyone's standards. It does not keep fresh as long as our own commercial variety, so it's best not to overstock.

Eggs—In all but the very smallest communities, the local citizens will have a few eggs to spare from their own flocks or from their market place. These are smaller than our U.S. hens' eggs, but this might be expected. Scratching is harder down there.

Beer, wines and liquor—Mexican Government cannery towns are not allowed by law to stock or sell any alcoholic beverages. This also applies to the Mission settlement of Mulege. For dependable sources of excellent Mexican wines, beer or rum, La Paz, Santa Rosalia, Loreto, San Jose del Cabo and Ensenada are, to our knowledge, the only suppliers. Resort hotels cater to bar customers but do not sell packaged goods.

Fruits, vegetables and staples (See "supplies available" in chart on page 76.) To answer the question, "Is it safe to eat fruits and vegetables grown in Mexico?" it may be noted that much of the farm produce (tomatoes, lettuce, semi-tropical fruits, etc.) grown in the lower peninsula area is exported to the southwestern United States. This could not be done if such imports did not meet U.S. Pure Food standards.

BOOKS AND CHARTS, BAJA CALIFORNIA

Cruising the Sea of Cortez, by Spencer Murray, photos by Ralph Poole. (Desert-Southwest, Inc., Palm Desert, Calif.)

Lower California Guide Book by Gerhard & Gulic; third revision (Arthur H. Clark Co., Glendale, Calif.)

Sea of Cortez by John Steinbeck (Viking Press: Compass paperback)

The Sea of Cortez, by Ray Cannon and the *Sunset* Editors (Lane Magazine & Book Co., Menlo Park, Calif.)

Many Mexicos, by Lesley Byrd Simpson (University of California Press, Berkeley, Calif.)

Kym's Guide #6, The Sea of Cortez and Baja Calif. Peninsula, by Ray Cannon (Triumph Press Inc., 320 E. Harvard St., Glendale, Calif.)

Sailing Directions for the West Coast of Mexico and Central America (H.O. #26)

Charts: Planning chart #1006 (Hydrographic Office) San Francisco to Manzanillo.

    # 619   Los Angeles Bay to northwest end of Gulf
    # 620   Loreto to Los Angeles Bay
    # 621   Magdalena Bay to Cape San Lucas and up to Loreto
    #2103   La Paz and Vicinity
    #1493   Ballenas Bay to Magdalena Bay

#1310   Cedros Island to Ballenas Bay
#1193   Bahia Rosario to Cedros Island
#1149   San Diego to Bahia Rosario
(Detailed charts of most of above areas are also available.)

RESORT HOTELS FOR INFORMATION AND RESERVATIONS

Bahia de Los Angeles:
1. Senor Antero Diaz, Apartado Postal 579, Ensenada, Baja, Calif., Mexico. Phone: Via marine operator through radio station KMI, Oakland, Calif., to the trawler *San Augustin*.
2. Hotel Punta Chivato: P.O. Box 6354 Sunkist Station, Anaheim, Calif. Phone: 635-7760

Mulege:
1. Club Aero Mulege, Mulege, B.C., Mexico.
2. Serenidad de Mulege: 4305 Donald Douglas Dr., Long Beach, Calif. Phone: 774-2257

Loreto:
1. Flying Sportsmen Lodge: P.O. Box 5588, San Diego, Calif.
2. Salvatierra #3, Loreto, Baja Calif., Mexico.
3. Hotel Oasis, Bill Benzinger, Loreto, B.C., Mexico.

La Paz:
For any hotel in area, International Travel Service, Suite 418, 510 W. 6th St., Los Angeles 14, Calif. Phone: MA 9-2666.

SE of La Paz:
1. Hotel Bahia de Palmas: 3630 Sunswept Dr., Studio City, Calif.
2. Rancho Buena Vista, C/O Chuck Walters, Box 1486, Newport Beach, Calif.

Cape San Lucas area:
1. Hotel Cabo San Lucas: P.O. Box 48747, Briggs Station, Los Angeles, Calif. Phone: 655-4760.
2. & 3. Las Cruces de Palmilla and Hacienda Cabo San Lucas, write: Las Cruces Palmilla, Box 1775, La Jolla, Calif. International (or other) Travel agency.

MEXICAN REQUIREMENTS FOR CLEARANCE OF PLEASURE BOATS

Pleasure boats entering Mexican waters are required by law (Article #191 of the General Communications Law) to be provided with proper clearance papers to be delivered at the first Port of Entry one puts into in Mexico. These forms, in quadruplicate, may be obtained either from a U.S. broker or from the Mexican Consular Service. The document must include: name and nationality of the vessel; destination; port of origin; full names of Captain and each of the crew (or guests) and the age, sex and nationality of each person aboard. Consular fees for this service are 200 Mexican pesos or U.S. $16.00. Mexican Consul or broker will also provide necessary forms for fishing or hunting licenses.

Before re-entering United States waters from Mexico, it is necessary to obtain a departure clearance from the last port of call in Mexico. This can be done at La Paz if it is planned to omit Cape San Lucas or Ensenada as ports of call on the return trip; or at Cape San Lucas if proceeding directly to San Diego; or at Ensenada if it is the last port of call. Such clearance papers are not required by the United States Customs Service, but serve the purpose of officially removing the yacht and its crew from the list of those still cruising in Mexican waters. The cost varies between $15.00 and $3.00, depending upon whether the clearance is obtained by a broker or by the skipper. When entering the United States at Shelter Island, San Diego Customs Station's interest concerns merchandise being brought in from Mexico, the absolute absence of any plants, fruits or vegetables aboard, the nationality of owners and guests.

ELECTRIC AND ELECTRONIC EQUIPMENT

With the exception of trailed boats, both power and sailboats will find an electric anchor-windlass a near necessity, because in all of Baja California there are no docks or slips for visiting boats, and the best of ground tackle is extremely important. Of equal value are a depth sounder and marine radio. Especially for the short-handed crew, an automatic pilot is of importance in reducing the work load for those on watch. Due to the limited number of broadcast stations and radio beacons in Mexico, direction finders are of only nominal value. Radar is useful for nighttime navigation and for use during the occasional periods of fog along the Pacific side of the peninsula.

SPARE PARTS—ENGINE OR SAIL

Caution: Carry aboard as much spare equipment as possible. To date there appears to be no easy way to receive in Mexico any parts ordered from the United States to be sent down to a Mexican port.

FILM

Do *not* send exposed film back to the U.S. from Mexico for processing. It rarely if ever is received in this country by the laboratory.

IMPORTS

Merchandise—each person clearing Customs back into the U.S. is allowed $100 worth of duty-free merchandise. Save your receipts for proof.

Liquor—California State laws forbid entry of alcoholic liquor purchased in Mexico if brought in by private pleasure boat or by private airplane.

AIR TRANSPORTATION TO BAJA CALIFORNIA AND FERRY

Aeronaves de Mexico Airlines, departing from either Los Angeles International Airport, or from Tijuana, Baja Calif., Mexico (situated just across the Mexico/U.S. border).

The M. S. La Paz ferry-cruise ship plying between La Paz and Mazatlan, makes two trips a week in each direction, departing from Mazatlan at 5 p.m. Tuesdays and Saturdays; and from La Paz on Thursdays and Sundays. Fares begin at $4.00 each way in

Salon Class with reclining chairs. Tourist Class passengers pay $16 for passage including a bed in a two- or four-berth cabin. For $28, passengers in Cabin Class are provided with double cabins, private bath and use of smoking salon, bar, dining room and swimming pool.

FISHING CALENDAR

San Felipe and vicinity

Totuava (large croakers weighing up to 300 lbs.)	Best during spring spawning runs, March into June
Sailfish, marlin and dolphinfish	Late June to December

Loreto and vicinity

Amberjack	October to May
Cabrilla	All year
Garropa	All year. Best in spring and early summer.
Marlin, Sail and Dolphin	May to November
Red Snapper and Roosterfish	October to April
Sierra	November to June
Tuna	June to November
Yellowtail	December to June
Miscellaneous game fish	All year

Coast and Gulf

Langusta (Mexican lobster) can be trapped on the Pacific side of the peninsula but on the Gulf side they have to be speared or taken by hand. For some reason they won't enter a trap in the Gulf.

Cape Area

Marlin	All year. Best May to August and November to February
Wahoo, Roosterfish, Tuna and Yellowtail	All year. Best May to August and November to February

MARINE WEATHER REPORTS

For weather reports in Mexican waters, most skippers rely on marine radio transmissions from commercial fishing boats or other yachtsmen cruising the area. For those who understand rapid Spanish, Mazatlan Radio broadcasts a weather sequence on 2715 kc's at 9:10 A.M. and 11:10 A.M.; also on 2660 kc's at 12:00 noon. (Mazatlan's time zone is the same as U.S. Rocky Mountain time.)

FUELING AND WATERING

The only harbors at which fuel and water are available from docks are La Paz, Cape San Lucas, Puerto Cortes in Magdalena Bay; Black Warrior; Cedros Village on Cedros Island; and Ensenada. In La Paz, fresh water is available at the Municipal Pier, after obtaining a permit from the Port Captain. A special pipe fitting is needed consisting of a male nipple threaded for 2″ pipe and with a reducer to accommodate a standard garden hose fitting, to which a length of hose of at least 50 feet must be furnished to get water into the boat tank. Diesel fuel is obtained from the oil company docks at Prieta Point, about 4 miles out from La Paz at the entrance channel. Again a permit is required from port officials. At the other harbors named, fuel and water is obtained at the same docks, and no hoses or special fittings are necessary.

Even though gasoline and diesel fuel are shown as available at certain harbors on the chart on page 76, there are times when supplies are exhausted by local fishermen and it may be necessary for visiting yachts to wait until the coastal supply ships arrive with new supplies.

At Las Palmas, fresh water is obtained through a long hose floated out from the beach to boats at anchor. The limited amount of gasoline available must be brought out in drums on a skiff, and pumped from the drums. At all other harbors where limited amounts of gasoline and water are available, the visiting yacht must provide the necessary hoses and have a hand- or electric-driven pump to transfer the gasoline or water to boat tanks. For that reason, separate hoses for fuel and water should be carried aboard to avoid contamination, and preferably, separate pumps.

FENDERS

Without exception, the skiffs and canoas of local fishermen are heavy, rugged boats without gunwale guards. This obliges visiting yachts to have many substantial fenders for hull protection. The most practical are automobile tires, covered with sack-like canvas bags to avoid black tire marks on hull sides. The average yacht fender, suitable for stateside usage, is far from adequate.

MECHANICAL AND HULL REPAIRS

At Santa Rosalia, La Paz and Ensenada, there are machine shops able to perform most engine repairs. There are marine railways at both Santa Rosalia and La Paz able to handle yachts of up to 100 tons gross weight; the ways at Ensenada are limited in capacity, although there is a modern floating drydock capable of handling vessels of up to 200 feet in length.

Machine shops are also available for emergency repairs at each of the cannery harbors: Cape San Lucas, Puerto Cortes in Magdalena Bay, Asuncion, Turtle Bay and Cedros Island village. The shops associated with the salt-mining operations at Black Warrior are also able to perform emergency repairs on visiting craft. Minor repairs could be made by local machinists at Loreto.

At La Paz, Electronica Arechiga, S.A., is qualified to repair electrical and electronic equipment, although their problem is generally the lack of spare parts if replacements are necessary. Lorenzo Verdugo M., Madero & Bravo No. 206, is recommended for engine repairs.

TYPES OF BOATS SUITABLE FOR BAJA CALIFORNIA CRUISING

Although an 18-foot outboard cruiser has successfully circumnavigated the peninsula, starting from Los Angeles and ending the trip at San Felipe, this is not recommended. Similarly, 20- to 22-foot sailboats have made the trip down the coast, proving that it can be done. In general, however, powered or sailboats of up to

25 feet in length should limit their cruising to the upper part of the Gulf. Launching points would be from San Felipe or Puertocitos on the Peninsula side, or Guaymas or Kino on the mainland side. Fuel, water, provisions and general comfort of the crew are the limiting factors.

There are hundreds of sport-fishing boats under 30 feet in length operating from Bahia Los Angeles, Mulege, Loreto, La Paz, Las Cruces, and from resort hotels at the Cape. The majority were either built locally, shipped down on the decks of freighters, or launched from trailers at the upper end of the Gulf and powered on down the Gulf. Their radius of action, however, is normally confined to 25 to 50 miles from their respective home ports.

Auxiliary powered sailboats of 30-foot length or more, and equipped with larger fuel and water tanks than normally provided, have only a few more problems than they would have in cruising stateside waters. The distances between provisioning stops, lack of ice for refrigeration and relatively long distances between harbors on the Pacific side of the peninsula are the principal ones. Forty-foot diesel-powered cruisers, with sufficient fuel for at least 350 miles of sustained cruising, are entirely adequate for cruising the Gulf regions but would need to pick their weather when going up the Pacific side of the peninsula. The longest jump between refueling points coming up the coast from the Cape, is between Magdalena Bay and Cedros Village, approximately 275 miles.

Our cruising in the Gulf has been aboard diesel-powered craft of 68 feet length or larger. Since virtually all harbors will accommodate deep-draft yachts, it is axiomatic that the larger the boat, the more comfortable and pleasant will be the trip. Our first *Monsoon*, commissioned in the mid-40's, was an ex-Army rescue craft of 104 feet in length. Originally these vessels were powered with three high-powered gasoline engines, and all auxiliaries were gasoline engine driven. Even if we had owned an oil company and could have afforded gasoline as fuel, which we certainly did not, the 3000 gallons of gasoline would have been adequate for only 300 to 400 miles of cruising. Hence, we repowered the ship with three diesel engines and diesel-driven auxiliaries, which gave us a range of 1500 miles at 12 knots.

Handling of the ship was strictly a team operation. We did not install pilothouse controls for many reasons, and used the original telegraph system between pilot house and engine room. A flip of a coin at the time we commissioned the ship resulted in the *Monsoon* being the only ship on the Pacific Coast with a female engineer. Her job was the handling of the three main diesels, all auxiliaries, and an electrical distribution panel large enough for a small city.

Our present cruiser, *Monsoon II,* commissioned by us in the mid-50's, is 72 feet in length, twin-diesel-powered, and on long cruises accommodates four in two large double staterooms with two spare bunks in the fo'casle. Her cruising range is about the same as our first *Monsoon,* and at 11 knots she can safely cruise 1500 miles between refueling stops. Electronically she is better equipped, having radar, automatic radio direction-finding equipment, in addition to autopilot, depth recorder and two radio telephones. With pilothouse controls, Chief Engineer Carolyn is now Skipper most of the time, and what little attention the engine room needs is now the duty of the Commodore.

Monsoon II has been particularly equipped for easy operation by the two of us, with full instrumentation in the pilot house, automatic alarm systems, and intercom communication between various parts of the ship. Even a full-sized fireplace was built into the deck-side main lounge to add to comfort and convenience.

One of the most important assets that we had, and have, aboard both ships is an inflated rubber life raft for going ashore. Wooden and fiberglass tenders are not basically designed for beaching through a surf, which is often necessary at some of the more exposed anchorages.

APPROXIMATE DISTANCES IN NAUTICAL MILES
BETWEEN PRINCIPAL BAJA CALIFORNIA POINTS

			Cumulative distances	
				To
	BETWEEN		From San Felipe	San Diego from
#1	#2	Miles	to col. #2	col. #1
San Felipe	Puertocitos	40	40	1438
Puertocitos	Willard Bay	40	80	1398
Willard Bay	Refugio	45	125	1358
Refugio	Los Angeles Bay	40	165	1313
Los Angeles Bay	San Francisquito	46	211	1273
San Francisquito	Santa Rosalia	72	283	1227
Santa Rosalia	San Marcos Is.	18	301	1155
San Marcos Is.	Mulege	20	321	1137
Mulege *	Loreto	66	387	1117
Loreto	Puerto Escondito	12	399	1051
Puerto Escondito	Agua Verde	25	424	1039
Agua Verde	Nopolo	35	459	1014
Nopolo	La Paz	62	521	979
La Paz **	Muertos Bay	55	576	917
Muertos Bay	Las Palmas	20	596	862
Las Palmas	Los Frailes	28	624	842
Los Frailes	Cape San Lucas	45	669	814
Cape San Lucas	Magdalena Bay ent.	160	829	769
Magdalena Bay ent.	Asuncion Bay	180	1009	609
Asuncion Bay	Turtle Bay	75	1084	429
Turtle Bay	Cedros Is. village	32	1116	354
Cedros Is. village	San Martin Island	155	1271	322
San Martin Island	Colnett Bay	32	1303	167
Colnett Bay	Ensenada	70	1373	135
Ensenada	San Diego, Calif.	65	1438	65

* Mulege to Guaymas	85
Mulege to Keno	110
** La Paz to Pichilinque	7
La Paz to Mazatlan	240
La Paz to Esperitu Santo Is.	24

PART II

CRUISING CALIFORNIA, OREGON AND WASHINGTON

CHAPTER 1

Broad Aspects

Topographically the California, Oregon and Washington coasts make a slow change from the dry, treeless shoreline of Baja California. The first 200 miles northward from the California–Mexican border only slowly become greener and timbered, and not until past San Francisco do winter rains and higher-moistured air give life to foliage.

The coasts of both Baja California and the United States have a common characteristic of a substantial mountain range close by the Pacific shoreline—sometimes rising 2000 to 3000 feet within a mile of the beach; other times further inland only as far as 5 to 10 miles.

Between San Diego and Eureka, California, a distance of about 630 miles, the coastal range and higher mountains of the Sierra Nevada range are separated by the vast Imperial and San Joaquin valleys. This has a distinct bearing on summer wind and fog conditions along this portion of the coast, with high heat in the valleys creating a strong draft of cool ocean air to flow into them as hot air rises from the valleys during the heat of day. This is followed by the warm air spreading out to the coast during the night and creating fog conditions that will persist until midday when the strong on-shore winds again take over.

Northward of the California–Oregon border, summer heat in the interior is not as great as in California, and there is less of a draft created. It is partially due to the more northerly latitude; more timbered mountains, which tend to hold down the interior temperatures; and smaller valleys, eastward of the coastal range. The result is less fog during July, August and September at such points as the Columbia River entrance in Oregon and Cape Flattery, Washington, than off such California points as Pt. Reyes and Pt. Sur. The *Coast Pilot* reports that during the three months of July, August and September the total fog-signal opera-

Point Arguello points a menacing rocky finger from shore.

tion at San Diego averages 20 hours for the three months, at Los Angeles, 101 hours, at the entrance to San Francisco 331, at Eureka 517, at Columbia River Lightship 189, and at Cape Flattery 373. This is in contrast to roughly 60% fewer fog-hours during May and June when inland temperatures are considerably lower. Similarly, the amount of fog during the early fall is considerably less than during the three summer months, for the same reason.

When making a northbound coastal trip many purposely do so in either late spring or early fall, to avoid the consistently higher northwest winds and morning fogs that are common during summer months. Those who do cruise north during midsummer will frequently take departure from one harbor to the next in the very early hours of the morning—long before daylight—and pass by such headlands as Pt. Conception, Pt. Sur, Pt. Reyes, Pt. Arena and Cape Mendocino as early in the day as possible to avoid the midafternoon winds that whip around these points. Small commercial fishing boats often hug the shore on the theory that the hills and bluffs tend to lift the strong flow of air at a distance of

Fog moves in suddenly over southern California waters. On this particular early-summer day we left Newport Beach, guided by radar, in zero-zero conditions, only to emerge later into clear skies about 8 miles offshore.

¼ to ½ mile from the beach—and thus reduce its velocity close by the shoreline.

Along the roughly 1200 miles of Pacific Coast that separate San Diego and Seattle, there are four major boating areas. The largest is between San Diego and Santa Barbara, which includes Newport, Long Beach and Los Angeles. Blessed with fair weather for most of the twelve months, this region of 175 miles length has more harbors than any other similar stretch of the Pacific Coast. Their development has been directly related to the density of population, which makes them economically feasible, although their year-around boat usage has contributed substantially to new harbor construction.

Second major boating center is in Puget Sound, Washington, with Seattle, Tacoma and Olympia the principal subcenters. While Southern California has as its main boating asset favorable weather conditions for open ocean sailing and cruising, the Puget Sound area's asset is its thousands of miles of protected waterways, hundreds of islands, and untold numbers of anchorages or mooring facilities.

The third boating center can be broadly described as in the

Monterey Cypress trees, known only to this area, shown here at Monterey Peninsula, west of the city.

triangle formed by San Francisco, Sacramento and Stockton, California. Here the many assets include some 1500 miles of rivers and connecting waterways of the Delta area, and the broad expanses of San Francisco and San Pablo Bays. These areas enjoy favorable boating weather for the majority of the year, and a larger number of small craft marinas and launching sites has been constructed within this triangle during the past five years than in any other area on the Pacific Coast.

Not to be overlooked is the boating activity on the Columbia

River, which separates Oregon from Washington, and its tributaries. Starting near the mouth of the Columbia River at Astoria, these cruising and sailing waters extend eastward to the manmade lakes that have been created by the building of Bonneville Dam and others, on either the upper Columbia River or its tributaries. Some 500 miles of cruising waters are in this area.

Between San Diego and San Francisco, roughly 425 miles, there are harbors or sheltered anchorages that make it an easy trip. The longest stretch between them is only about 50 miles—between San Simeon anchorage and the lee of Pt. Sur. Eight of the harbors are new within the last five years, man-made by dredging millions of cubic yards of earth from the shoreline and building jetties to form entrance channels.

North of Pt. Reyes, 25 miles northwest of the entrance to San Francisco, the distances between harbors or sheltered anchorages jump to between 75 and 150 miles. Going further north, along the Oregon and Washington coasts there are such harbors as Coos Bay, Waldport, Newport, Tillamook, Astoria (10 miles within the entrance to the Columbia River), Willapa Bay and Grays Harbor. Some of these are not more than 20 or 30 miles apart, but each is at or near the mouth of a river. Without exception there are bars to negotiate at the entrances. Under fair weather conditions there is no problem of crossing the bars, but they are tricky or downright dangerous if seas are running. Those who do go into the Oregon and Washington harbors along the coast should time their arrivals at the entrances to be in the mornings, and preferably during slack- or flood-tide conditions.

It has always been our choice to make a direct run between Port Orford and Cape Flattery. The distance is about 340 miles, but one completely avoids the problem of bars at the intermediate harbors. The only time that we did not make a straight through-run was when it was necessary to enter Gray's Harbor, on the Washington coast. Although it was reasonably calm off the coast, the Coast Guard advised us to wait nearly six hours for the start of the flood tide into Gray's Harbor before crossing the bar.

Once around Cape Flattery, the northwesternmost point of Washington, it is a downhill ride through the Strait of Juan de Fuca to Puget Sound or the Strait of Georgia in British Columbia waters. The mountains of Washington and Vancouver Island are timbered down to the water's edge on either side of the 15-mile-wide Strait. Scores of coves, bays and harbors—such as Neah Bay just 8 miles inside Cape Flattery—offer excellent

Jones Island, San Juan Archipelago.

anchorage after the long and sometimes rough trip up the coast.

At a point roughly 75 miles eastward from Cape Flattery, the equally pleasant decision must be made whether to turn south into Puget Sound, or north toward the San Juan Islands. Thousands of miles of shoreline and hundreds of islands are in an area that measures only about 100 miles on its north-south axis and 50 miles in width. Here, the rigors of deep-sea cruising or sailing can be forgotten and exchanged for smooth sailing, great fishing and anchorages too numerous to count.

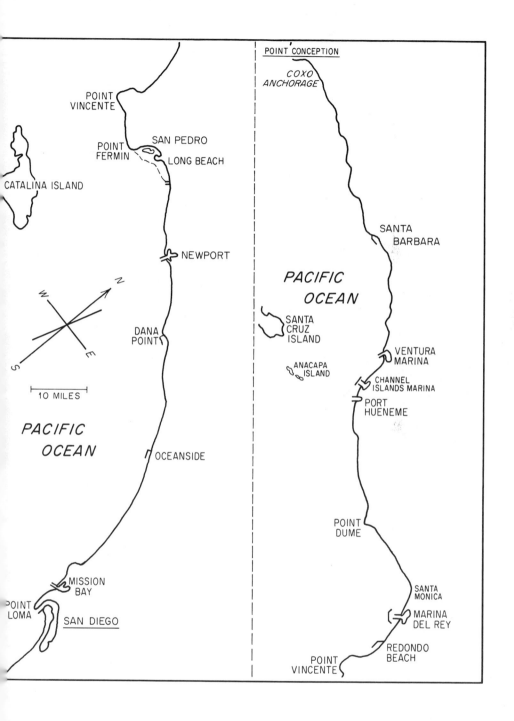

CHAPTER 2

San Diego to Santa Barbara

When Juan Rodriguez Cabrillo first sailed his ship into San Diego Bay in 1542 there is no reason to believe that he was particularly carried away with the sight before him of miles of tidal flats, water acres of kelp and only the scrubbiest of brush ashore. But it was a natural harbor of sorts, and a fairly protected anchorage under the headland of what is now Point Loma. Even after Junipero Serra founded his Mission at San Diego 227 years later, the harbor remained in its primitive condition for another hundred years. Actually most of its tremendous improvements have been made in this century, the most recent of which have favored the fishing fleet, a Naval base and users of pleasure craft.

Today, San Diego's boot-shaped bay has been dredged and molded to allow for 25 square miles of navigable waters. A focal point for pleasure boats is the $1,300,000 man-made peninsula called Shelter Island and the newer Harbor Island, soon to be finished, and also formed from local dredging spoils. Shelter Island is studded with fine restaurants, hotels and docking facilities for many of San Diego's pleasure boats. It also offers a free launching ramp which has served over 1200 launchings in one six-hour period. Harbor Island, now landscaped and ready for building construction, will provide 127 acres of useable water area for slips and access.

San Diego Harbor's Unified Port District has looked wisely into the future needs of pleasure craft in many ways. One aspect, important to the itinerant yachtsman who may not be a yacht-club member, is the availability of guest slips. Should these facilities be full, the San Diego Harbor Master will endeavor to direct the visitor to an alternate slip or mooring. Slip rentals in the area run from $.70 to $1.00 per foot of boat length, compared to a charge of up to $1.75 per foot made at many other southern California marinas.

San Diego's Shelter Island looking northerly. Customs and Harbor Master's docks in lower foreground. Southwestern and San Diego Yacht Clubs are on west side of harbor, Silver Gate Yacht Club and four marinas on east side. At extreme upper right is new Harbor Island yacht basin.

Glorietta Bay, the southern segment of this vast San Diego Harbor complex, serves the communities in and around Coronado—site of the venerable (circa 1884) Victorian-styled Coronado Hotel and its picturesque Boat House. Practically any type of craft is available for hire here and at Shelter Island: sailboats, skiffs, motor boats and fast speedboats with water-skiing equipment. Throughout the year daily excursions may also be taken in either conventional sightseeing boats or in highspeed hydrofoils. One of the most noteworthy of the many boating contests hosted by San Diego is the 1400-mile, non-stop Acapulco sailing race which is held on alternate even-numbered years.

Five miles north of Point Loma lies Mission Bay Park, another

Boathouse adjacent to the venerable Coronado Hotel, Glorietta Bay, San Diego.

swamp-to-swank Aqua Park encompassing 2500 water acres, three major marinas and half a dozen luxury hotels overlooking the water. Because of its vast size and purposeful design a full gamut of water activities may be engaged in, each in its own designated area—swimming alongside sandy beaches, water-skiing, casual day-sailing, fishing and speedboat racing. Quivira Basin is designed as a large-boat marina and along with its complete facilities, fuel, service, restaurants and hotels, it has easy access from its mooring area to the ocean. This basin has 500 (toward an ultimate 1200) slips available and, like others in Aqua Park, maintains ample guest slips for overnight mooring. Free anchorage is permitted in Quivira Basin for a period of up to seventy-two hours.

In one section of this huge Aqua Park at Mission Bay, where a total of 12,000 slips will be built as needed, is the entertainment center of *Water World* patterned after the *Marineland* enterprises of Los Angeles and Florida. Whale and porpoise shows, Japanese pearl divers and other spectacles relating to marine life highlight this popular exhibition.

The foregoing brief description of these San Diego-situated marinas closely resembles that of the balance of Southern California's sophisticated pleasure-boat facilities. Space does not permit an itemization of the wealth of accoutrements offered boat owner and tourist at each of the subsequently noted southland harbors. For a list of book and chart sources containing such detail, see appendix to Part II, page 179.

Oceanside Marina, 30 miles up the coast from Mission Bay, is one of the southland's newest harbors, with slips for 600 boats, some of which are reserved for guest use. Oceanside's channel entrance is usable most of the year by average-draft boats, but silting has necessitated the use of dredges at fairly regular intervals to keep the channel open. During southerly blows, entrance and fairway waters are apt to be dangerous. Under these circumstances, one should check by radio with the Harbor Master on duty before attempting entrance or exit. Under usual favorable conditions, however, Oceanside Marina is a comfortable harbor, well endowed with both necessities and luxuries—from marine fuel to the quaint shops and hostelry of a New England-styled Fishing Village.

To interrupt the 33-mile span between Oceanside and Newport, a new breakwatered harbor at Dana Point is rapidly nearing completion. Occupancy will commence in late 1971.

Mention is made of this harbor-to-be (of which Dana Point is but one of three projected for 1975 completion in southern California) chiefly to emphasize that definite steps are being taken to relieve a full-to-capacity situation which now prevails at many of these southland marinas. Waiting lists for slip occupancy (which run into the hundreds in this state alone) are decreasing as each new harbor facility is completed. And through trial and error, more functional engineering methods are being employed toward creating sound, economical bases for each succeeding year's crop of new boat owners.

Since 1934, the Newport Harbor/Balboa Bay boating mecca has expanded to make room for approximately 7000 boats. The area contains nine yacht and sport-fishing clubs and a host of fine restaurants which provide slips for their water-borne customers. In fact, if there is any enticement missing for the pleasure boat owner, either in Newport or in its eight southern counterparts, it might be only a little more cruising or sailing space within harbor confines.

With so many boats congregated in a relatively small area, visitors may ask: "Where do they all go? What do they do?" True, there is not the multitude of quiet, forest-fringed coves of

Looking westward from Los Angeles Harbor to 20-mile-distant Catalina Island, beyond which can be seen San Clemente Island. Eighteen yacht and small-boat anchorages provide mooring for approximately 5800 boats in this area comprised of San Pedro, Wilmington and Terminal Island, lower left.

seclusion available for our southland-based boats, such as New England and the Northwest offer in abundance. But choices in abundance remain for this southern fleet's water-borne entertainment. Trailed boats enjoy both ocean-going and smooth-water adventures in the State's inland lakes. Hot-boat speed races entice their aficionados to full summer and fall scheduled events. Predicted-log power-boat contests and sailing races are on the agenda throughout the year. Meanwhile, high on the list of fun afloat for almost all types of boats are the harbor-hopping holidays enjoyed between southern ports and the offshore islands of Catalina, Anacapa and Santa Cruz. Ocean fishing goes on all year with the anglers' greatest excitement culminating in late August at the start of the marlin run. Christmas lighted-boat parades, character-boat parades, opening-day parades . . . scarcely a week of the year is without some special event being held for spectator or boating participant.

The Fisherman's Fiesta is an annual event of the commercial fishing fleet based at San Pedro, Los Angeles Harbor.

The only glaring difference among southern California's marinas, other than variance in size, is in the availability of overnight guest moorings. It is ironic that Los Angeles Harbor, the largest Pacific Coast port, has no accommodations for the transient pleasure boat. Yacht club reciprocal guest privileges are of course the answer to "where do I tie up?" for club members in the Los Angeles area, but the non-club member has a real problem. There are a dozen privately operated yacht anchorages in Los Angeles Harbor, all of which are crowded with permanent tenants. Only Los Angeles Yacht Club could offer other club members a possible moorage or end tie, space permitting. This sad state of affairs is especially troublesome when the Trans-Pacific or other major sailing race is scheduled to depart from Los Angeles Harbor. Requests to private slip owners for overnight tie-up start months before starting day for these races. Likewise, those vacationing on their boats must attempt to reserve a slip or mooring, at such points as are necessary on their itinerary, weeks in advance of departure from home port. Maybe

The clean skyline of Long Beach, viewed from a portion of the land fill that forms the entrance to its large commercial and pleasure-boat harbor. The boat in the left foreground is a "one-design" of another era.

they will be assured of a berth or maybe not, depending on how crowded the marinas are during the vacation interval.

The best solution to this problem, as far as Los Angeles Harbor is concerned, is to suggest that the visiting boat turn to nearby Long Beach Marina at Alamitos Bay where end ties are kept open for visiting boats. Facilities there are of the finest, and ample guest space is available at a reasonable charge for as long as a fifteen-day period each month.

Looking on upcoast from Los Angeles Harbor, there are four more marinas in this 82-mile span before one reaches Santa Barbara: King Harbor at Redondo Beach, Marina del Rey, Channel Islands Harbor at Oxnard and Ventura Marina. Of these, King Harbor does keep a few end ties open for visiting boats in the 30-40 foot class, but giant-sized Marina del Rey, for all its multi-million dollar cost, turns a $figurative$ back on guest boats. Marina del Rey's three yacht-club tenants have a few slips available for other club members' boats. This still helps neither the large-boat owner nor the non-club member. Anchoring is for the most part frowned upon. There is, however, twenty-four-hour Harbor Master service headquartered at the marina administration building (to starboard for incoming boats). A mooring or slip request from this department could possibly prove fruitful should a permanent tenant's boat be away—from any of the half-dozen privately operated facilities in this enormous marina complex, ultimately destined to base 6000 boats.

After leaving Marina del Rey, on a westerly heading upcoast, one passes the indentation of Santa Monica, which fifty years ago was expected to become the State's greatest commercial port. But its open roadstead situation soon proved that breakwaters were entirely inadequate to stand against the continual hammering of wind and storm-built seas. This thundering surf is welcomed, however, by an increasing horde of surfers who frequent the several mile stretch of sandy beach fronting Malibu, which adjoins Santa Monica to the west.

Before long the headland of Point Dume is visible to starboard, beyond which are more bright sand beaches. Paradise Cove lies 2 miles northeastward of the Point with a series of similar coves spotted at intervals along this shoreline interval. These coves are ringed with kelp and are used primarily by small boats. They are not suggested as overnight anchorages.

Point Mugu, 15 miles west of Point Dume, is a large Navy missile-testing station. Consequently the waters surrounding the area are frequently designated danger zones for boats traveling in the vicinity. Notice of missile firing schedules from Mugu are broadcast to mariners Mondays through Fridays at 0900 and 1200 hours on 2638 and 2738 kc's. When such firing is occurring boats must follow alternate courses as advised by the Navy.

A mile before reaching Channel Islands Harbor is Port Hueneme (Y-nee-mee) an important Naval base and semi-commercial port. If in distress a pleasure boat would be allowed refuge in this harbor, but otherwise yachtsmen are requested to use either of the adjacent harbors at Oxnard or Ventura, which lie only 8 miles apart. Channel Islands Harbor is noted as a sportfishing center; it offers charter or rental boats and has available a launching ramp and the usual array of marina facilities. Despite frequent dredging in this entrance channel, rapid silting occurs along the north side of its entrance channel. Boats moving into the harbor should therefore hug the opposite jetty.

Ventura Marina, too, has its share of silt insidiously building up at its channel entrance, ever since its breakwaters and jetties were completed in 1963. The silt situation is indeed one of many problems besetting Pacific Coast harbor designers and engineers. But until the solution for eliminating this incubus has been found, dredges keep busy around the clock and boats continue to fill the harbors they keep open. Many of Ventura's new slip tenants are coming from as far as 50 to 80 miles away to enjoy Ventura's marina facilities, plus its advantage of proximity to the offshore islands of Anacapa and Santa Cruz.

While cruising the 13-mile coastal span from Ventura to Santa Barbara, shoreside scenery takes on a subtle change, with intermittent patches of green now relieving the bluffs and mountainsides. And ½ mile off Punta Gorda, a new island appears to have suddenly risen from the sea. Its tall stand of palm trees sways in the wind, its aspect that of a south sea atoll. This is Rincon Island, man-made by offshore oil well drilling interests, camouflaged in respect to its surrounding beauty, but in no way resembling the natural offshore islands dimly discernible to sea.

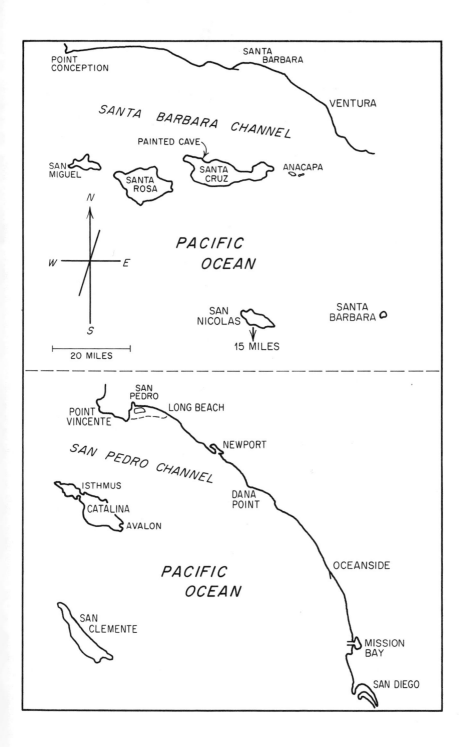

CHAPTER 3

California's Offshore Islands and Painted Cave

Despite weather statistics compiled in *Coast Pilot* concerning numbers of "fog hours" per month and related data, residents of southern California will agree that since 1962, each spring and early summer month has had successively less and less sunshine. The months of May and June have always been notorious for overcast and little wind, but this same static condition is now extending well into July and August. It is therefore suggested that late August, September and October are best months of the year to enjoy cruising these southern ocean waters. At this time, water temperature averages 70 degrees and weather settles down to a fairly dependable forecast of "light variable winds in morning hours, becoming northwest, 10 to 20 knots in afternoons." For boats afloat in the Catalina or Santa Barbara channels, this means smooth-water cruising early in the day and good sailing winds for afternoons, plus an all-day opportunity to upgrade the suntan.

Scattered from 11 to 53 miles offshore between Los Angeles Harbor and a point beyond Santa Barbara are eight islands which, if combined, would comprise an area approximately a third the size of the state of Rhode Island. Locally termed "the Channel Islands" they are best known to the sailboat fraternity and to United States Navy and Air Force personnel who man the various island bases as part of our Early Warning System.

Scarcely a month of the year passes without a major sailing race scheduled from the mainland shores out to and around one or more of these lonely yet historic islands. Prevailing channel winds present the greatest of challenges when those with stout boats and crews use these natural pylons as outer markers for their oft' beyond-hull-speed contests. These are the races that separate novice from experienced. There's little chance of becalmed periods out there, where winds can reach gale-force peaks at any time of year.

Winds of lesser velocity may be found around others of these islands, situated more closely to the mainland, but times are rare when the sailing vacationer is not assured of a brisk run to Catalina, Anacapa and Santa Cruz Island. In the power-boat field, outboard hot-boats have held annual 'round Catalina Island races for the last several years, with start and finish line at King Harbor, Redondo Beach. And in 1965 the West Coast's first 180-mile Long Beach-Hennessy Offshore Power Boat Race was held, starting at Long Beach, past the east end of Catalina to San Clemente's west end, around that island to the west end of Catalina and back to Long Beach. This grueling run, patterned after the famous Miami-Nassau power boat race, had both local and Eastern entries vying for cash and trophies.

Historically, islands have always been known to "beckon" the sailor, but of these eight offshore chunks of land, only Santa Catalina Island may be visited ashore without permission from either private ownership or the government—and even Catalina owners now require a small landing fee for shoregoing at any cove except its one commercial community of Avalon. Even so, as the number of pleasure boats increases in the state, so rises

New Year's morning in Catalina Harbor, the nearly landlocked bay on the Island's ocean side, opposite the Isthmus anchorage. Each New Year's holiday a group of two to three dozen boats sail or cruise to this popular island harbor to enjoy the usually balmy weather, afloat.

the number of people visiting the three remaining accessible islands—if not for shoregoing, at least to lie at anchor in some of our last remaining peaceful quiet coves.

Geologists and archeologists inform us that in the Wisconsin Ice Age, some 45,000 years ago, all of these eight islands were probably a part of the mainland when an estimated 20,000 Canalino Indians made the coastal section their home. Perhaps that tribe had its own type of Early Warning System to protect them from warring enemies' spear missiles and from the roving mammoths, bones of which are still being discovered on these windy island shores. Other artifacts unearthed in kitchen middens and at burial sites have disclosed that the Canalinos had a highly developed culture before they were assimilated by mainland Indian tribes of lesser intelligence, and before the era of the missions which followed Cabrillo's arrival in 1542. Jesuit padres brought the Canalinos to the mainland to "educate" them and this marked the beginning of the tribe's end. Now only hawks, ravens and pinnipeds (sea lions and sea elephants) carry on an island lineage commenced so long ago.

Most recent settlers to all but Catalina, Santa Barbara and Anacapa Islands are the military. The geographical sites of these outposts make them ideal for such missile-firing practices and radar-tracking projects as are necessary for linking our western defense chain. Thus, San Clemente Island is now off-limits for the pleasure boat owner. Before its restriction in the late 40's we recall many pleasant cruises to this 18-mile-long island— where giant pink abalone show themselves at low tide and where fox and wildcat used to scurry from our children's shoreside campsites. Once they used a hand fog-horn to scare the wildlife from their campfire. Now Navy aircraft booms a grim admonition to a more menacing adversary.

Twenty miles southwest of Los Angeles Harbor lies Catalina Island. Although its summer season is becoming more crowded yearly, it remains the most popular of the island group primarily because of its proximity to the state's highest-density pleasure boat area. Secondly, there are more than a dozen summer children's camps spotted at convenient intervals along the island's lee shore. Although there are occasional winter storms, for most of the year the channel waters from mainland to island are benign enough to permit a crossing by the smallest of craft. At Avalon and the Isthmus harbors there are restaurants, fuel and such shoreside entertainments as are appealing to (or necessary for,

Typical summer scene at Catalina Island's Isthmus harbor. One may hike less than ¼ mile across the Island from this point to Catalina Harbor, the only protected anchorage on Catalina Island's ocean side.

as the case may be) its many seekers. Catalina Harbor, nearly landlocked, also provides an ample calm-water anchorage for boats taking the longer run around to the windward side of the island. Almost every major Catalina cove is the site of a yacht-club facility while other club groups have dining and play areas ashore for their members' seasonal use. Public transportation, both air and water, carries thousands of summer visitors to famed Catalina—the one island of the offshore group which may be termed a "spa."

Westward of Catalina some 28 miles is the chain's smallest island—Santa Barbara, a black, rocky hump rising to a 600-foot summit. Except for two unattended navigational lights, the island appears nearly barren during most of the year. Due to heavy kelp ringing its perimeter, a landing is virtually impossible. Most of the commercial fishing boats frequenting this area rely on their kelpcutters for negotiating these exceptionally rich fishing grounds; and they in turn are of the privileged few who see Santa Barbara at its glorious best during springtime. In early April the giant coreopsis burst into bloom, sending their golden sunflower-like blossoms up 6 to 8 feet high, a brilliant mass of color often visible 10 miles distant. And it's in order to perpetuate this singular flower and other waning species of flora and fauna that the Channel Islands National Monument was created in 1938. Thus these unusual plants, as well as birds and sea-mammals previously headed for extinction, are now under National Park protection for their perpetuation.

Further westward 24 miles is San Nicolas Island, completely off-limits to all but the military. Despite this outpost's violent winds and blinding sandstorms (or perhaps *because* of the elements' hostile nature) one of the world's largest concentrations of sea elephants and sea lions congregate and propagate. Sharing these desolate shores, lobster and all classes of abalone—pinks, blues and blacks, cling to their eroded rock homes—rocks so hole-ridden they appear to be hard gray sponges. Although skin diving is not allowed, the government personnel manning their San Nicolas station are welcome to this bountiful shellfish so long as it is taken only at lowest tide level. "They call this the poor man's Catalina," one of the officers laughed, "but I'll take our grub any day rather than a snow cone or hot dog!"

The last two of the Navy and Air Force base islands of Santa Rosa and San Miguel lie well to the northwest of Santa Barbara on the mainland. Both islands share a unique historical possession of dwarf-mammoth bones unearthed by archeologists. It is assumed that when these original pieces of mainland fell away to become islands, the mammoth colonies became inbred and eventually stunted. Neither Island has much to attract pleasure-boatmen.

Santa Rosa, the chain's second largest, does have several anchorages that may be used by yachtsmen, providing missile firing or other exercises are not in progress at their base. A huge crane near the government dock provides a cage lift for service men and cargo to be hoisted some 70 feet from their boats to the station high on the rocky hill above, indicating the nearly inaccessible nature of this island's shoreline.

Turning back toward the mainland, the Anacapa Islands lie offshore 11 to 16 miles southwest of Port Hueneme and the two previously described marinas at Oxnard and Ventura. Usually referred to as one island, the Anacapas are actually a narrow line of mountain peaks, forming three separate islands as they rise abruptly from the ocean floor. Here the sea has honeycombed the shoreline into arches and caves where, at intervals, surge builds up astronomical pressure beneath surface rocks, only to spout a resounding geyser of spume from recessed blowholes.

Anacapa's habitations consist solely of a Coast Guard lighthouse and radio-beacon station on the eastern island, and a one-man-maintained Forestry Service camp on the center portion, whose duties are concerned with the National Parks wildlife program. The access beach to the Forestry camp lies on Anacapa's eastern shore, and during prevailing winds its anchorage is protected and has good holding in 3 to 5 fathoms.

From atop the narrow island's center, a view down the razor-back ledge is an awesome sight. Breakers slam unceasingly against windward cliffs, relentlessly disintegrating its lava base, forming new arches, eroding older formations. Historians say the Canalino Indians called the island "Eneeapah," meaning "changing" or "deception," and pronunciation's evolution brings us "Anacapa."

One of our most memorable visits to Anacapa and Santa Cruz Islands was a group cruise, with six other boats joining us, whose primary purpose was to inspect and photograph the interior of the Painted Cave on Santa Cruz Island. We had aboard with us our friend Milt Farney, who was making a television movie of the channel islands, and it is to him we are indebted for these accompanying illustraions of the two islands and the inner cave.

Although Santa Cruz island is privately owned, one wishing to visit ashore may do so from Prisoner's Harbor westward, providing he secures a permit from the owner (see Appendix to Part II, page 180). Such permission prohibits the boatowner from taking firearms or pets ashore, and its purpose is understandable from a view of preserving island wildlife and the remaining stands of evergreen trees, oaks and succulent undergrowth. From Prisoner's Harbor east are situated a Navy radar tracking station and other government operations which are restricted from the general public.

Surge is the dominant obstacle in the Painted Cave area, so our little expeditionary force felt extremely fortunate in having a rare calm morning and flat seas for our venture into this cavern. Due to extreme water depths which prevent anchoring near the cave entrance, we left our vessels moored in Cueva Valdez cove, which lies only a few miles east of Profile Point and Painted Cave, and proceeded west in our dinghies. Milt brought all manner of lighting equipment, Frezzo-lites, magnesium flares and torches, without which it would have been impossible to illuminate even partially the stygian blackness of the Cave's inner recesses.

At its 150-foot-high entrance the grotto appears to be spattered

Exploring the Painted Cave, Santa Cruz Island, by small boat. From the entrance, shown here, the cave tunnels back approximately 300 feet into utter darkness.

with vari-colored paints. Iron, zinc and copper strata mingle their corroded colors with brighter tints of sea lichen, and cave-nesting birds add their daubs of white to complete this natural mural. Colors dimmed as we ventured further underground where the ceiling slants down to an eventual infinity—300 feet back at the cave's bitter end. We shut off our outboards and paddled, trying to glide along as quietly as possible in order not to scare the seal colony which we knew inhabited the dead-end beach. After the faint shaft of entrance light had been cut off by a bend in our watery corridor, we were in a darkness impenetrable beyond belief. From the dank rocky overhead came a drip, drip of moisture while eerie noises emerged from unseen blowholes. Our voices echoed hollowly. A seal's sudden bark startled us all, tensed as we were for the unexpected.

Milt was especially hoping to photograph an albino seal who, with his dark-haired family, had appeared briefly with the first flash of his Frezzo-lite. But before we could focus our cameras there was a tremendous snorting and splashing and at the next beam of light, only one tiny seal was left in view. Apparently too young to fear us, he blinked, bewildered, but clung to his rock. Meanwhile the adult mammals were swiftly making for the outer ocean, no doubt terrified at the sight of seven boats, twenty-five people and what was probably the first bright light ever to illuminate their home.

Despite smoothest of seas that day, surge inside the Cave measured up to three feet in rise and fall, giving us little head room at the end of the cavern. Tide was on the rise and smoke from our torches commenced to thicken the air. "One more picture, please . . ." Milt pleaded, "then you can get out."

Eventually out in clear air and open ocean, we turned our motors up to full bore and raced back to our ships for a long over-due breakfast and a chance to stretch our legs ashore. Later in the afternoon one of our little fleet's skippers hauled in his fishing line to find attached a 10-foot killer shark! Needless to say, our swimming after that was confined closely to shore.

Later in the week we leisurely cruised the Island's perimeter, with overnight anchorages at such harbors as Pelican Bay, Smugglers' Cove, Chinese and Fry's Harbor. At Lady Harbor we hiked up to its natural "bathtubs" where spring water gurgles through fern and moss, rushes over boulders in tiny waterfalls, finally to fill to brimming three stone basins each the exact shape of a bathtub.

Pelican Bay is a favored anchorage on the northeast side of Santa Cruz Island.

Whether climbing the Island's bluffs or contemplating this panorama from the sea, always some indications remain of early island days: a dilapidated ranchhouse, a vineyard's skeletal remains, the silver-gray order of a onetime fig orchard, now dead and bleaching on a windy slope. From Indian to European to bird and animal kingdom—so the island's rule was transferred. Now another era has commenced with most of the channel islands lending their vantage points to our national defense. Perhaps the day is imminent when these offshore outposts will either be closed in their entirety to pleasure boating or, more likely, turned into massive housing projects. Whatever may be their future, those of us who have taken our boats to their primitive shores and can still do so today are indeed thankful that we could heed these islands' beckoning.

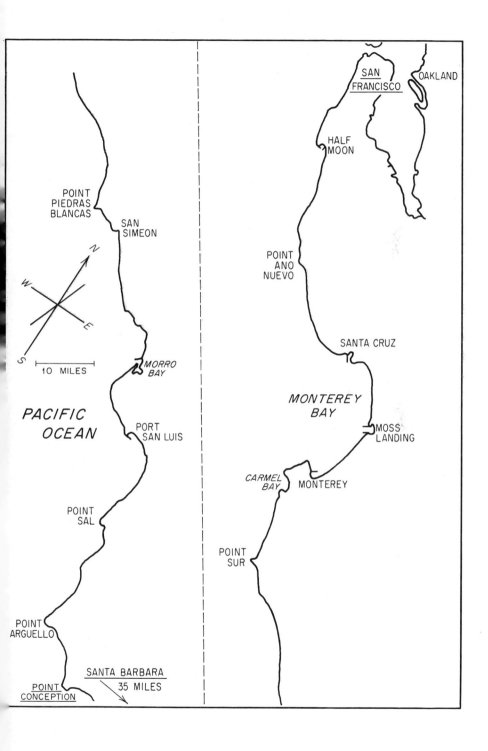

CHAPTER 4

Santa Barbara to San Francisco

Santa Barbara's harbor is important to the north-bound yachtsman in several respects. For those with limited cruising range it serves as a last fuel and supply depot before commencing the sometimes arduous, 90-mile run upcoast to Port San Luis. Its proximity to Santa Cruz Island, 20 miles offshore, presents a fine sail or power cruise for either day trips or extended vacationing. And perhaps most important, Santa Barbara is a gay and festive community with shoreside enticements reminiscent of its historical background during Spanish and Mexican rule.

Two of the most notable festivals held annually here are *Semana Nautica* with its scores of sailing races, regattas and all manner of marine contests and exhibitions, during Fourth of July holidays; and the *Old Spanish Days Fiesta,* enjoyed during the full-moon week of August. The latter event tells in parade and pageantry of Santa Barbara's changing years since its discovery by Cabrillo in 1542, its official christening by Vizcaino in 1602, on through its tenure as Presidio and Mission Center, to present days. Probably no other coastal city has cast its allegiance to as many flags as has Santa Barbara: the flag of the Spanish Empire of Carlos V was first to wave in 1769; the Spanish National Ensign, from 1785; flag of the Mexican Empire of Iturbide, from 1822, and of the Mexican Republic, from 1824; the California State Bear Flag, superseded by the 28-star American Flag, was raised in July 1846, and finally its Official City Flag and the Star-Spangled Banner with its present field of 50 stars.

Although much of Santa Barbara's former vast ranch holdings have since been divided many times, much of her former heritage still remains in evidence in architecture, and to a lesser extent in custom. It is actually one of the West Coast's few cities which appears, in a figurative sense, to have no visible means of support. Rather than a backdrop of smokestacks, factories and high-

The ceremony of Cabrillo's landing in the Santa Barbara area in 1542, and his claiming the land in the name of the King of Spain, marks the opening of Old Spanish Days, Santa Barbara's annual August fiesta.

rise business structures, only the rich green heights of Santa Inez Mountains tower behind harbor and town, as if to isolate them from the grubby mechanics of industry. This is primarily a summer place, a wintering spa, a sanctuary for retirement, higher education and the arts. Thus bemused, no great effort has been spent on harbor maintenance, although a small dredge is operated most of the year to clear the entrance channel of its continuous silting. But once inside the breakwater, a visiting boat and crew receives the most gracious attention. In all but southerly storms the harbor provides good protection for its 700 boat-slip tenants and visiting craft. Early summer weather is for the most part overcast during morning hours with gradual clearing by afternoons. Generally, day-long sunshine commences in late August or September and prevails through fall and early winter.

Of our many cruises into Santa Barbara and on up the coast to San Francisco, all have been quite different with respect to weather, sea conditions and facilities encountered at shoreside. For this reason it would be difficult to call any one of such cruises "typical." Rather, we will recount a group-cruise in which we participated, to point up the fact that boats in the 30-foot class can cover this span, often with aplomb equal to that of their larger cruising companions.

Early in July of 1965 a dozen boats joined forces to cruise together from San Diego to San Francisco with overnight stops planned at intervening harbors. By a direct course the distance is 426 miles, but our more devious harbor-hopping route took us 500 nautical miles. We were a heterogeneous fleet, reading from small to large: a 35-foot diesel-powered Monterey, a 38-foot Chris-Roamer, a 40-foot Huckins sport fisher, a 40-foot ketch-rigged motor sailer, several cruisers of from 48 to 63 feet and our own 72-foot *Monsoon II*. As this will indicate, no two boats were alike in design or in speed, and over half the group had not taken their boats this far northwest before. But we were well organized as to plans and equipment, and all had radiotelephones for intercommunication at frequent intervals. Slower boats— those cruising 7 to 9 knots—planned their starting times earlier than those with faster cruising speeds, and radar-equipped boats acted as leaders for those without the "seeing eye." Because dense fog was the order of the day for the first three days such radar leadership proved a definite asset for all concerned. But with the fog came a cessation of wind, resulting in just about the smoothest seas we had ever experienced offshore along this coast.

By our fourth day out, sunshine finally broke through. Only two boats of our fleet had had to return to their home bases (due to a time element rather than to mechanicals); crews had become well acquainted, and all were getting their sea legs. Most days saw us gathered in ports long before sundown, visiting each other's boats and later joining for dinner at yacht-club or marina restaurants. (It is worth comment here, in reference to earlier statements concerning a lack of guest slips at various of the southland marinas, that it was a part of our planning to arrange in advance for both slip and dinner reservations at those harbors on our itinerary.)

Boats of our fleet with lesser fuel capacities stopped at Santa Barbara to top off their tanks, and our fourth night's rendezvous brought us to Coxo (or Cojo) anchorage, just to the northeast of

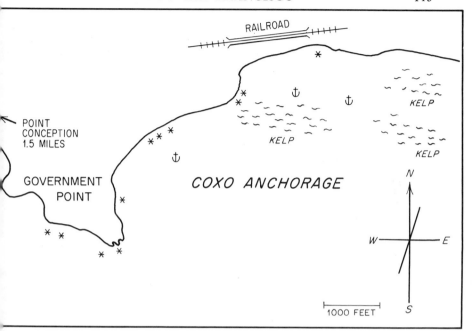

RAILROAD

KELP

POINT CONCEPTION 1.5 MILES

KELP

KELP

GOVERNMENT POINT

COXO ANCHORAGE

N

W —— E

S

1000 FEET

COXO ANCHORAGE
34 deg. 27 min. N. lat.
120 deg. 27 min. W. long.

Anchorage at Coxo is in relatively shallow water, from 2 to 5 fathoms, and preferably between the heavy growths of kelp and the northerly shore. The bottom is hard sand. Some parts of the kelp are so thick that caution should be exercised to find open paths through it. These openings change position from season to season, but are generally discernable as routes through smoother water where kelp is thickest. Prevailing summer winds from the northwest whip across Point Conception and Government Point, generally from noon until sunset, and more than the usual amount of scope should be paid out after setting anchor. When winds are from the northeast to southwest, there is no protection from them in this anchorage. There are no facilities ashore at Coxo and the amount of surge normally precludes access to the beach. Breakwaters close by Government Point are planned for this anchorage, as a part of a harbor of refuge program. They will give protection during all wind conditions.

Point Conception. This small bight, protected to some extent from north and west winds, has been used for many years by pleasure and fishing boats as a harbor of refuge but it is utterly untenable in south or easterly winds. Point Conception has long been known as the "Cape Horn of the Pacific," and those who have seen the elements rage around this 200-foot-high eminence agree that the name applies. We felt fortunate in finding calm weather when our flotilla moved into Coxo's proection that evening. Ashore there is nothing but tawny, lion-colored bluffs, empty of tree or habitation—only a train runs at intervals along the lower shoreline. The sound of its passing strikes a strange discordant note against the mumbling background sound of surge and surf. An actual harbor, with breakwaters and slip facilities, is in the planning stage for Coxo; but until that becomes reality, we can sit at anchor contentedly, watching the sunlight fade across the dark-gold hills, listening both to the surf and the train, hooting off in darkness around the bend of "Cape Horn."

Our fleet weighed anchor early the following morning, anxious to put as many miles as possible behind us before early afternoon winds arose. Ocean swells were big but not breaking as we rounded Point Arguello, 12 miles beyond Point Conception. Regular seafarers along this route have also called Arguello by other than its true name. One of its (less-offensive) appellations is "Graveyard of the Pacific," since it was often the scene of destruction for ships plying the steamer lanes in earlier days. The most tragic loss occurred in 1923 when seven United States destroyers followed one another to their destruction on the fearsome rocks offshore Point Arguello.

During this fifth day's run, some of our group stopped at Morro Bay for fuel while others ran straight through to our second "anchorage-only" stop of the trip, at San Simeon Bay. Our own ship was scheduled to stop briefly at San Luis Obispo Bay to pick up a friend. When we did so, their kindly Harbor Master and his wife presented us with a beautiful, freshly caught salmon and two loaves of homemade bread! Such is the kindliness and generosity so often manifested at many of these less-populated ports.

Port San Luis with its adjoining city of Avila has been, through the years, primarily a fuel depot for tankers, as well as an occasional haven for the fishing fleet. But now after long and diligent work by San Luis Harbor Commissioners and with necessary local backing, the area will soon become a well-breakwatered harbor and marina for pleasure craft. At the time of writing it is only an anchorage, and its ancient pier becomes increasingly derelict as it extends into the Bay; but by 1970, the first phase of work is expected to be complete at this harbor, with slips for small craft, convenient fueling stations and the usual array of restaurants and supply shops ashore.

Morro Bay's harbor, 21 miles beyond Port San Luis, offers its small-craft patrons many of the accouterments associated with the large marina. Its primary deficiency is its narrow entrance channel, which scarcely allows more than single-file exit or entry into the nearly landlocked harbor. The Coast Guard maintains a station here; fuel and top-quality restaurants are handily adjacent to the limited slip and anchorage area. Caution should be used in anchoring due to the 4- to 5-knot tidal currents caused by the constriction of ocean flow in and out of Morro's narrow channel.

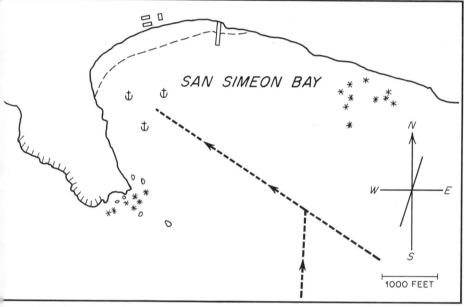

SAN SIMEON BAY
35 deg. 38 min. N. lat.
121 deg. 11 min. W. long.

This bay provides good protection from prevailing northwest winds and sea, although a moderate surge is almost always present. A lighted buoy is to the southeast of the point and should be kept to port when entering the bay, due to the reef and kelp which extends from the point toward the buoy. Best anchorage is close under the wooded bluff in the western portion of the bay, in 3 to 6 fathoms of water. The sand beach looks inviting, but generally there is too much surge breaking on it to make practical the beaching of the average dinghy. The vertical ladder at the end of the fishing pier is most often used if it is necessary to go ashore for supplies or to telephone. No fuel or water is available at the pier. A breakwater extending northeastward from the point is planned, along with other developments that will ultimately include full facilities for local and visiting craft.

Once visitors are securely moored, Morro Bay offers a variety of diversions, including golf on its stately tree-studded grounds overlooking the harbor and ocean fishing or clam digging along its several "sand islands" (which soon may be dredged away to allow more mooring space). Due to Morro Bay's geographical position and certain attending meteorological conditions, winter months are warm and generally sunny, but from June to September overcast skies and fog are the rule. None of this bothers the ardent fisherman, and both commercial and sport-fishing craft use the harbor to good advantage all year.

Our little armada consisted of eight boats when we moved into San Simeon Bay to anchor for the night. High on the hilltop overlooking the Bay, famed Hearst Castle stands a lonely sentry, guarding its Midas-wealth of art treasures. The Castle's western windows glitter in late afternoon sunlight; its high twin towers thrust upward against a deep blue sky. A tour to and through this baronial treasure house is certainly a rich experience, as evidenced by the thousands of visitors who have been guided through its grounds and museum-like buildings. But this safari is one to be made from a point on land—from the small crossroads of San Simeon or from 18-mile-distant Morro Bay to the south. The only shore access at San Simeon Bay is up a high vertical ladder attached to a fishing pier. Only rarely will surge permit any sort of a shore landing in the average dinghy carried by pleasure boats.

The five of us aboard *Monsoon II* had, we are certain, the finest dinner of our entire trip that evening while anchored in San Simeon Bay. We baked our gift salmon in foil where it poached in its own juices to a mouth-watering perfection. We logged that interval "night of the salmon" and felt a little guilty that our other fellow cruising companions could not share our feast.

As weather and seas build their own mosaics of contrast, we had all felt uneasily that our sea lanes had been quiet unusually long. So it was with no surprise at next early dawn that we headed out of the Bay into increasingly turbulent seas. On the hour we called and talked with each of our fellow skippers, and their answers of "all's well" were reassuring. Our admiration grew, particularly for the Tuttles in their 35-foot Monterey—such a small boat for these huge swells building up around Point Sur! In contrast to California's more southerly points, this bold headland is thickly forested down its many perpendicular valleys.

Hearst Castle, a unit of the California State Park System, San Simeon, Calif.

The community of Big Sur is home to a growing art colony and other settlers who seek this picturesque privacy that lies betwixt towering evergreens and the breaker-bangled sea.

By early afternoon we were abeam Carmel and Pebble Beach's ocean-fronting golf course; rolling past the lovely shoreside vista of Cypress Point, Spanish Bay and Point Joe—all scenic and historical landmarks on Monterey's notable Seventeen-Mile Drive which winds overland from Carmel to Monterey Bay. Monterey

Typical of the rugged shoreside scenery around Carmel and Monterey Peninsula is this view of Cypress Cove, Lobos State Park, Calif.

was once California's Capital, when the territory was under Mexican rule, and like Santa Barbara it retains much of its early-day flavor. Many of its old adobe buildings have been restored and are open to public viewing.

Alerted to our arrival, Monterery's Harbor Master came out to the breakwater to meet each of our fleet to guide them to an inner-harbor slip. And from that moment on, we were treated as royal guests by the friendly, hospitable people of Monterey. We were invited to a succulent sea food dinner that evening by members of Monterey Yacht Club, and those who wished to see the city were invited to tour some of the historical sites and buildings now rejuvenated through the efforts of Monterey's Historical Society. One of the most venerable of these early adobes is the area's first Customs House, originally built in 1814.

Our next day's cruise was a short one, across 22-mile-wide Monterey Bay to its north shore harbor of Santa Cruz. This is more of a resort town than is Monterey, but it shares much of the same turbulent history under foreign rule. Interspersed with the new are scores of homes and commercial buildings built in the early 1800's. Protected as it is from prevailing northwest winds, Santa Cruz enjoys a warm summer climate. Its long stretch of sandy beachfront and many summer cottages welcome visitors throughout the season. Pleasure craft are drawn to the newly finished marina which provides launch and drydock areas and well-built slips for over 300 boats. The breakwater entrance does leave something to be desired, however, and for a boat with over 5 feet of draft the channel should be negotiated only during high tide.

We had an exciting roller-coaster ride into this channel— poised momentarily atop a huge rolling sea, then plunged downward while the undertow swept out behind us; pouring on the

Twenty-seven-ton Quadrapods are used in breakwater construction at Santa Cruz Harbor. Of French derivation and first successfully used in the Mediterranean, they were later manufactured in this country, and as Tetrapods were employed at the breakwater in Crescent City, Calif. Advantages of the pods include elimination of slippage due to their legs' interlocking action, and an increased porosity of the breakwater structure.

power to maneuver around the narrow dogleg—some fast maneuvering to avoid Sunday's sailing sabots—and finally to steerage way and quiet waters, not to mention reduced pulse!

Once again the welcome mat was extended us, by Santa Cruz Yacht Club members and others of their Harbor Commission. Ideally situated in a bower of great old trees and facing the harbor marina, the Yacht Club was the site of a delightful dinner held for our fleet from the southland. Later, cars were put at our disposal by local friends—an especial boon to those having boat shopping and laundry to take care of.

Moderate fog prevailed during our 46-mile run up the coast from Santa Cruz to Half Moon Bay (sometimes referred to as Pillar Point Harbor), our last anchorage before our arrival at San Francisco. Only a few years ago, Half Moon had millions of dollars expended on breakwaters to protect its harbor; slips and mid-basin fueling stations were constructed, all with the expectation that these would provide a safe and functional marina for the fishing fleet and for pleasure craft. But before the first year was out, winter storms slammed in and over the new breakwaters, destroying slips and floats, and sinking seven of the boats that were moored inside. As with a number of other harbors to the south (such as Ventura, Marina del Rey, King Harbor and Oceanside) remedial steps were necessary to make Half Moon a safe harbor. An extension to the westerly breakwater was constructed to overlap the original entrance. Since then no further problems have been experienced. Despite the lack of slips, fuel is available from the dock which withstood the storm.

After a good night's rest we were all up early to run our last 24-mile lap to San Francisco. Departures were planned so that each boat would meet promptly at 1000 hours under the Golden Gate to pass through in formation.

At 0955 hours, as *Monsoon II* neared the bridge, we found ourselves a little ahead of the rest of the fleet. In order to drop back into line, we started a wide 360-degree turn; but no sooner were we well into our turn than we saw, to our great amazement, that all the other boats in our group were also doing little circles of their own! "Well," they told us later, "we were just following our leader."

We have since wondered what other ships' crews thought of us while we were making circles right in the center of San Francisco's busy channel. Perhaps it's better that we never know.

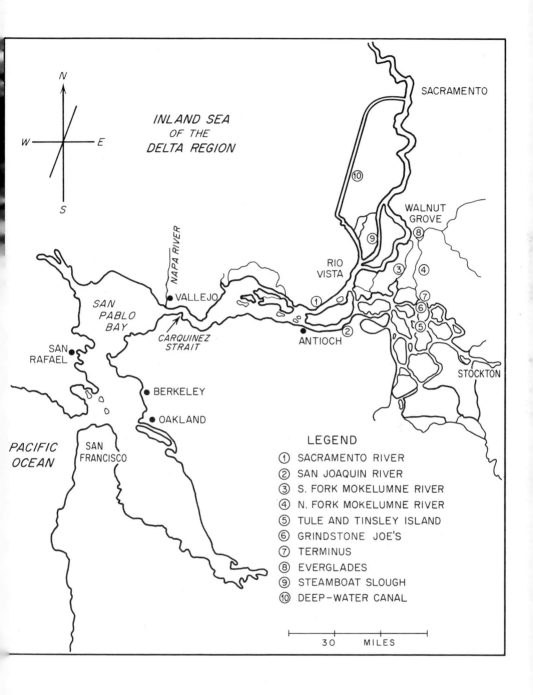

INLAND SEA
OF THE
DELTA REGION

SACRAMENTO

N
W   E
S

⑩

WALNUT
GROVE

⑨   ⑧

NAPA RIVER

RIO
VISTA

● VALLEJO

SAN
PABLO
BAY

③   ④

⑦

①   ⑥

CARQUINEZ
STRAIT

⑤

② ANTIOCH

SAN
RAFAEL ●

STOCKTON

● BERKELEY

● OAKLAND

PACIFIC
OCEAN

SAN
FRANCISCO

LEGEND

① SACRAMENTO RIVER
② SAN JOAQUIN RIVER
③ S. FORK MOKELUMNE RIVER
④ N. FORK MOKELUMNE RIVER
⑤ TULE AND TINSLEY ISLAND
⑥ GRINDSTONE JOE'S
⑦ TERMINUS
⑧ EVERGLADES
⑨ STEAMBOAT SLOUGH
⑩ DEEP-WATER CANAL

30   MILES

CHAPTER 5

The Inland Sea of the Delta Region

An interesting feature of the San Francisco Bay area is the fact that one may, in effect, select the weather simply by cruising a few miles one way or another. As one moves eastward from the windy Golden Gate and enters the protection of San Pablo Bay, temperatures rise, humidity falls and summer reigns supreme. Prevailing summer fogs at the Gate are usually nonexistent three or four miles eastward and it is into this warmer climate we now turn.

The Delta region covers over 700 square miles with 1500 miles of waterways in central California where its superbly rich peat soil annually produces millions of dollars of foodstuffs for its landowners. Now oil is being pumped from the farmlands, adding to the productivity of an area once known only for gold mining.

Our course takes us past Alcatraz Island, famous for many years as one of the major federal penitentiaries, but now closed; its destiny remains a point of argument for city, state and federal officials. A turn toward the north puts beautiful Angel Island and the Belvedere-Tiburon residential area, on the northwest side of San Francisco Bay, on our port side before reaching the wide San Pablo Bay. Close study of the charts is necessary along the northeasterly courses crossing San Pablo Bay, because definite channels must be followed to avoid shoal water. Twenty-five miles out of San Francisco Bay puts us abeam the Navy's Mare Island at Vallejo on the Napa River. Established in 1854, Mare Island is still one of the Navy's largest bases for drydocking and overhauling.

Before continuing through Carquinez Strait we swing into the Napa River, passing close by the Navy Yard, under two bridges and into the meadows through which the Napa River quietly flows. Our intent is to visit the wine-producing community of

128

Sailing enthusiasts seldom lack wind in San Francisco Bay. Shown above, the 35-foot *Touché* practices a spinnaker run under the Golden Gate.

Napa, using the outboard tender, if necessary, for the shallow upper reaches of the river. (A "caution" on the charts was well stated. As we passed Slaughterhouse Point, a group of fishermen waved to us with what appeared to be a friendly greeting. However, their waving was a warning that the channel was now some distance to the west of our present course, and we were soon hard and fast on the bottom. Fortunately the mud was soft and the tide was rising. An enforced wait of a couple hours saw us underway again, this time back toward Carquinez Strait, rather than pressing our luck by going to Napa.)

It is from this point inland that a Delta cruise begins to take shape and color, particularly in the fall, when the 500- to 750-foot-high hills flanking the Strait are mantled in reds and golds of wild grapevines. Benicia is at the eastern end of the Strait. Rusting skeletons of abandoned gold dredges still lie on the shore to remind us of the California Gold Rush in the 1850's. Just past Benicia there is another reminder of history—a spot at which more than four hundred decommissioned ships of various types used in World War II are neatly moored, twenty abreast and many rows deep.

The next ten miles are a series of channels through Suisun Bay, well marked with buoys and echo boards. Low, tule-covered islands lie to port as we move up the channel to Pittsburgh, facing the New York Slough. River traffic at this point is mainly ocean-going freighters, or tankers traveling to Stockton or Sacramento; oil- and produce-carrying barges pushed or pulled by tugs; sail and power cruisers headed toward or returning from the Delta. The waters between San Francisco and Pittsburgh,

Bridges along the Sacramento and San Joaquin Rivers are kept busy opening their spans for summer recreational boat traffic. Most commercial vessels have used the Sacramento Deep Water Channel (not shown) since its opening in 1964.

roughly 40 miles, are not too good for outboard boats because the broad reaches can be mean and choppy.

Turning up the San Joaquin River, we enjoy the hospitality of Bridge Marina at Antioch, which is similar to many of the marinas along the rivers. Generally they consist of a narrow cut in the riverbank, at right angles to the stream, which then opens into a fine group of covered moorings, gas docks, fishing and marine supply stores and generally a restaurant. The Bridge Marina is one of the more extensive. Maneuvering 72 feet of deep-draft ship within some of these marina basins is not always easy, because the majority are built for cruisers of 30 to 45 feet in length.

Destination of the next day's run is Potato Slough, to visit with a group from San Francisco which will rendezvous at a point marked "x" on our chart. The deep-water route from Antioch to Potato Slough is up the San Joaquin River, but instead we take a "cross-country" route via False River, past Frank's Tract. False River connects with the San Joaquin about ten miles above Antioch and it wanders leisurely through farm lands.

Frank's Tract, which we pass while enroute to Potato Slough, was once a famous farm holding but near the turn of the century the dikes ruptured and it flooded. On the chart is the notation "temporarily submerged," and it will undoubtedly continue to be so for years because it has become one of the more popular fishing and hunting areas, with scores of shooting blinds, resorts and small-boat docking facilities.

From our rendezvous point with our San Francisco friends, we move farther up Potato Slough into Little Potato Slough and continue to Grindstone Joe's Landing. This is a private club, owned by a group of some sixty boat owners who maintain slips and an open-air clubhouse, unique for the Delta area.

Wanting to cruise the South Fork of the Mokelumne River, we head for Terminus where Little Potato Slough and the Mokelumne meet. Three blasts on our whistle, repeated a number of times, brings no action from the bridge that had to be opened to reach Terminus. Finally, we are hailed from shore and told that the bridge is opened only with twenty-four hours' advance notice during late fall and winter months. This is one of the few bridges in over 1500 miles of Delta waterways that are not almost always opened for cruising traffic. Still anxious to see some of the Mokelumne, we anchor *Monsoon II* and take to our dinghy, very much wishing we could get under the bridge with the ship. There are at least a hundred more miles of cruising beyond the bridge.

Again aboard *Monsoon II* we start downstream to the San Joaquin River, which takes less than two hours to reach even at half speed, then turn east toward Stockton. Enroute we visit Delta Yacht Club on Tule Island. They have excellent float facilities, with special television antennas, water and electricity. On a previous visit we noted with interest that their club rules included one which forbade the running of auxiliary generating plants after 10 P.M.—something more anchorages should enforce. Nearby, the St. Francis Yacht Club which is a San Francisco landmark, has its up-river facility on Tinsley Island. A narrow cut in the Island leads into a basin that has accommodations for upwards of 50 power and sailboats at floats, backed by an acre of green lawn, with swimming pool, barbecue areas, and a clubhouse converted from an abandoned lighthouse. At both the Delta and St. Francis Yacht Clubs the facilities are reserved for their members, although yachts home-based 200 miles or more away are extended guest courtesies, and generally can be accommodated during two- or three-day visits. A nominal charge is made by both clubs for overnight docking.

The distance from Tinsley Island to the inner harbor of Stock-

St. Francis Yacht Club's Tinsley Island facility is a popular rendezvous for visiting Club members, and for those who may have cruised up or down the coast a distance of 200 or more miles distant.

ton is about 10 miles. One is then within walking distance of the downtown portion of the city. As in the northwest, much of their moorage space is covered, but it is for protection from midsummer sun rather than midwinter rains. Stockton is the eastern end of the water highway, although small sloughs continue southward for a number of miles.

Retracing our course down the San Joaquin River toward its junction with the Sacramento River near Antioch, we wind our way through the Threemile Slough cutoff which saves nearly 25 miles in the trip to Sacramento. One sharp turn in the slough requires backing down on one engine while going ahead with the other, to swing the ship around a 270-degree bend; this also has to be done a number of times in the Georgiana Slough.

Once into the Sacramento River, at this point considerably wider than the San Joaquin, it is but a short run to Rio Vista, one of the oldest communities in the Delta. In contrast to some of the hundred-year-old buildings is the ultra-modern Delta Marina on the southern edge of the city. Like its counterparts in the Delta area, it has a narrow cut through the river bank which opens into a spacious basin with over 100 covered berths, slips for another 60 boats and a launching ramp. Fuel, ice, supplies, laundry facilities are available. A fine restaurant is on the river bank at the entrance cut, and a guest dock for larger visiting boats is on the Sacramento River side of the marina. Another ½ mile upstream, at the foot of Rio Vista's main street, is a municipally maintained float for visiting boats. Adjoining the float is a well-used small-boat launching ramp which is in almost constant use by owners of trailed boats, and water skiers. Many of Rio Vista's century-old buildings have been replaced by modern structures, one of which is Foster's Restaurant. Here, the owner has on display what is claimed to be "the world's largest private collection of big game trophies." We enjoy a delicious dinner at Foster's, under the hungry-appearing gaze of four hundred mounted animal heads.

Less than three miles upstream the waters split into three arms; the easternmost is the Sacramento, the middle branch is Steamboat Slough, and the one continuing northwestward is Cache Slough. The new deep-water canal for ocean-going ships enroute to Sacramento has its southern terminus a few miles up Cache Slough, then makes a beeline for 25 miles to the new commercial harbor on the west side of Sacramento.

It is a little startling to go from the ½-mile-wide Sacramento at this point into the narrow continuation of the river. The scenery likewise changes abruptly, with heavy growths of trees and shrubs lining the banks. The beauty of this portion of the Sacramento River is evidenced by the hundreds of summer homes lining its banks and the scores of small-boat launching ramps and docking facilities built around picnic grounds and public parks. At Walnut Grove the community's growing interest in boating is attested by a 150-foot guest float and a large sign welcoming visitors to the town.

A half-mile north of Walnut Grove is the small Chinese settlement of Locke, now only a remnant of the once thriving Oriental populace which helped build the levees during the late 1880's. The community was originally built on stilts over the marshes, its building three stories high. A century ago it roared with Tong

Locally known as the Delta's "Everglades," this bird and wildlife refuge offers an interesting cruise by outboard.

wars, gambling and opium dens. Now the buildings lean precari-
ously, grayed with time and weather. Only a few Chinese remain,
quiet and withdrawn behind a sheltering tangle of undergrowth
separating Locke from Walnut Grove and the nearby busy
highway.

Above Walnut Grove are the headgates of the Dela Cross
Channel through which water is released, during certain times of
the year, to irrigate large areas of the San Joaquin Valley. Behind
these huge gates and open to small boats only during low water,
is a primitive cruising area locally referred to as "The Everglades." A refuge for birds and game, it remains unmarked and
undredged. Great trees festooned with wild grape and moss arch
toward one another across the water, as if anxious to enfold the
unwary boatman. Sometimes their roots or deadheads do trip a
careless speeder.

With an outboard one can spend days on the Everglades' quiet
water trails. It's a silent place, save for bird calls or the occasional splash of jumping fish. Around a bend is an ancient houseboat with a sagging rocking chair at deck's edge—its fishing chair.
Another turn reveals a second houseboat, a $50,000 one, spar-
kling white and chrome against its dark green backdrop. One can
muse about their owners. The first started fishing here and stayed.
The other grubbed in his city gold mines to reach the status of
his neighbor—living on a houseboat, fishing, in a peaceful
hideaway.

The other entrance to The Everglades is through the Mokelumne River, which empties into the San Joaquin near Potato
Slough. Cruisers up to 40 feet in length can wind their way up
to a point behind Walnut Grove, but the going is slow and shallow for much of the upper reaches.

Continuing upstream toward Sacramento, we pass the upper
entrance to Steamboat Slough. Here we can usually find dozens
of power, sail and outboard boats anchored or tied to the river
banks, swimmers enjoying the sand beaches, and water-skiing
enthusiasts reveling in its midchannel. Commercial traffic does
not use Steamboat Slough, which is one of the reasons for its
recreational popularity.

One of the Delta rivers' most interesting shopping centers is at
Courtland, a community dating back to the mid-80's, on the
banks of the Sacramento. Good floats invite visitors to stop and
shop in its 75-year-old stores.

Almost imperceptibly the river narrows as it approaches the
State Capitol where there are a half-dozen excellent marinas. The

The peaceful quiet of Delta river-cruising provides an enjoyable change in pace from cooler and faster tempo of days afloat on the Pacific ocean.

Sacramento Yacht Club is built on a huge barge that will rise and fall as much as 20 feet with the change from low water to flood stages. The River View Yacht Club, beyond the bridges, has floats for 100 or more boats, and high on the banks over their moorages is a clubhouse made from an abandoned sternwheeler apparently beached during a flood. Marine railways large enough to handle the powerful river tugs and other boat repair facilities line the Sacramento's western banks.

Coast and Geodetic Survey charts end at Sacramento, as does much of the work of the Army Corps of Engineers in dredging and snag removal. Commercial and pleasure traffic can continue upstream for many additional miles, though, and annually the Stockton to Redding Outboard Marathon race goes northward nearly to the Oregon state boundary.

With unlimited time available one could extend his Delta cruising for many weeks, but time is marching on and this indulgence in smooth-water cruising cannot go on forever if we are to reach our northwest destination. So it is "all lines clear" and *Monsoon II* heads downstream, to the wider reaches of San Pablo and San Francisco Bays. There we refuel, replenish supplies and secure all gear aboard, ready for the wind-swept seas of the Pacific.

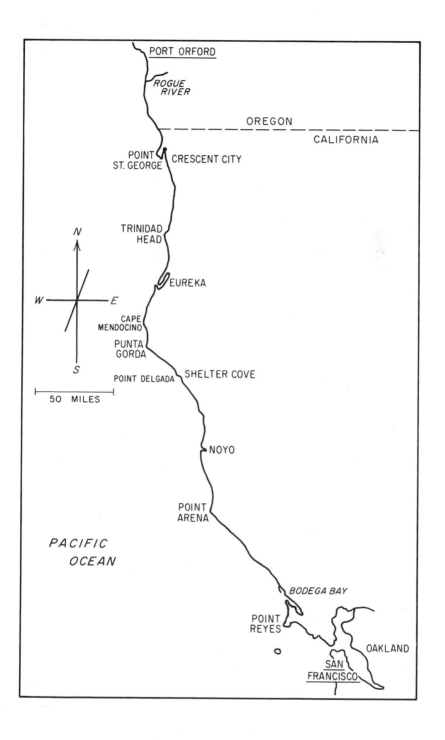

CHAPTER 6

San Francisco to Port Orford

Now we're headed out of San Francisco Bay, under the Golden Gate, usually into a noisy uproar: diaphone groaning, bell buoys clanging, whistles shrieking, each sound sending its individual warning to guide the skipper into his lane, outbound through what is locally known as the "potato patch." This section of choppy water extends roughly 3 miles beyond the bridge where shallow waters are more easily disturbed by wind and tidal change.

Through usual summer fog, the radar-equipped boat progresses contentedly, noting each buoy and ship within its vicinity and accurately gauging the distance offshore. To me, one of the most fascinating sights on the radar screen is that of approaching and passing under a bridge. At first there's the scanner's straight white line across our path—the bridge. Just as we reach this apparent barrier, an opening appears, like a little door, in the white line's center. Then the door closes after we have passed under the bridge. Behind us once more is that unbroken line connecting the two shores. (This of course applies to bridges *only*. A breakwater, for instance, would also appear in radarscope as a horizontal white line if we were headed directly toward it. A barrier that would *not* have a "little door" open for a boat heading into it!)

Once we're through the potato patch, on a westerly heading, Point Reyes lies ahead to starboard, the first of the many headlands to round before reaching the northern boundary of California. After leaving San Francisco there are a number of small coves and harbors one can use as rest or refuge anchorages before covering the 234 nautical miles to Humboldt Bay and Eureka. However, only a few of them have fuel available, and only two offer safe anchorage if winds are from the south. For this reason the wise skipper commences his northwest voyage with his vessel as fully founded as possible.

138

Named for Sir Francis Drake who first landed here in 1579, Drake's Bay is protected by Point Reyes and is the first of these possible anchorages after leaving the Golden Gate. In northwesterlies it provides good holding in 5 to 6 fathoms of hard sand. Fuel and water are available ashore. A Coast Guard station is maintained just inside the easterly end of the Point, which protection is chiefly used by the fishing fleet.

Twenty-three miles beyond Point Reyes, Bodega Bay offers a good anchorage in its northern extremity; alternatively, small boats can proceed through the 2-mile dredged channel leading from the Bay to the head of Bodega Harbor, where fuel and supplies may be had. Bodega was first settled in 1812 by a group of Russians who were hunting sea otters, which then proliferated

Looking down on Bodega Bay, lower left, and upper right, the small-boat harbor at end of 100-foot-wide and 9- to 12-foot-deep entrance channel. Bodega Harbor has a marine railway for boats up to 40 feet in length and 5-foot or less draft.

these shores. Other Russian migrants settled at nearby Fort Ross and along the Russian River. Fort Ross is now a State Historical Monument, preserving several homes and buildings of Russian architecture, built in the early 1800's. Long after most of the Russians and all of the fur-bearing otter were gone, Bodega Bay's small harbor became headquarters, during Prohibition, for rum-runners who were supplying such demands in San Francisco. The story is told of the coroner who drove almost daily from a dark night's rendezvous with boats in Bodega Bay to San Francisco and back, his hearse emitting gurgling noises as it careened along the highway. "Yup," quoth the coroner, "we're having quite a serious plague over Bodega way!"

From this point on up the coast, the mountainous shoreline becomes increasingly forested and a certain amount of debris may be found afloat. Logs or parts of trees are swept down the many rivers which empty into the Pacific. A helmsman should keep a watchful eye ahead.

From Bodega Bay there is no cove or harbor of any sort to the northwest until after rounding Point Arena, but 30 miles beyond this is Noyo anchorage adjacent to Fort Bragg, a total distance of roughly (in both senses of the word) 80 miles. Noyo is the principal fishing-boat center for this area, with some north and south protection in its small outer bay and a landlocked inner harbor for small craft.

On one of our trips up the coast a few years ago, we were experiencing strong head winds and extremely heavy seas, with weather deteriorating after we had rounded Point Arena. It was a case of throttling back until finally we seemed to be making more miles up and down than forward. On marine radio fishermen were talking about the lumpy seas and saying that "we're all blowed in . . ." to the nearest points of protection. We decided it would be well for us to do the same. A check of our charts showed the closest anchorage would be at Shelter Cove in the lee of Point Delgada. We had not been into that cove before, so Jack called on radio to one of the fish-boat skippers, told him that we were taking quite a beating, and asked for some detail about this anchorage, and whether it would be adequate for our boat's 7-foot draft.

"Sure, Cap'n," the skipper answered, "but there's a bunch of rocks and shoals in there. You want me to tell you the best way to go in?" Jack had just commenced replying to our unseen benefactor when we took an unusually big sea, part of which went

Noyo Harbor looking seaward. In foreground is new 265 boat marina. Supplies of all types, marine railway and repair facilities are available in this snug harbor.

down an engineroom ventilator, shorting out the motor-generator that powered our radio. The set was dead, and there was no way to finish our conversation with the fishing boat. Darkness was then falling and neither of us was interested in tackling a strange cove at night without knowing more about it. So we changed course a few degrees to port to clear Cape Mendocino and trudged on to Eureka. We have since wondered if the friendly skipper we'd been talking to thought we had foundered in the blow when our transmission was so abruptly chopped.

Twenty miles beyond Cape Mendocino and outlying Blunt's Reef is the river-bar entrance to Humboldt Bay and the city of Eureka. From Humboldt's river mouth on to the northwestern boundary of the United States, there is only one major coastal harbor that does not have a river-formed bar to cross; this is at Crescent City, near the northern boundary of California. So this is the time to dust off the tide tables and keep them handy for navigational reference, well in advance of one's entry into Humboldt Bay and all the Oregon and Washington coastal harbors to follow. The best time to cross any of these bars is during the last of flood tide. During the ebb, and with afternoon winds strong from the northwest, all of these bar entrances are seething cauldrons of tormented waves, often impassable even for large ships.

Eureka's Yacht Harbor lies 2 miles inside Humboldt Bay, and the city proper, another mile inland. All supplies and facilities that might be needed can be found here. Slips and docks are well maintained, and nearby are several picturesque wooded islands. In particular, an interesting dinghy tour can be taken around Gunther Island, which was the scene of a large-scale Indian massacre as recently as 1911. Indian arrowheads and other kitchen midden artifacts can be turned up almost anywhere around Gunther's grounds. We were fortunate in exploring the island when the Old Gunther House, a landmark since the turn of the century, was still standing. Not long afterward it was purposely destroyed by fire because, according to local citizenry, it had become an attractive nuisance. It was the typical "haunted house," long neglected, and with three levels of once-luxurious rooms to investigate. Gunther House was but one of the many historical structures on this coast with window glass, fixtures and fine hardwood panelings brought from the Atlantic Coast on sailing ships in the 19th century, around Cape Horn and up the Pacific Coast. In contrast to the many rugged ocean-miles that were covered in that era, and the hardships encountered during the establishment of new homes on this primitive coast, today's pleasure-boat cruises along these waters appear tame as Sunday sailing.

Trinidad Head, 18 miles up the coast from Humboldt Bay, is the next cove with good anchorage and protection from the northwest. During the summer salmon run this small cove in the lee of the Head is awhirl with activity, with fishing boats, skiffs and outboards dashing about in quest of their silvery catches. Charter fishing boats and hourly rental boats are available on a first-come-first-served basis.

Crescent City's harbor lies another 40 miles beyond Trinidad. This is mainly a commercial harbor for the export of lumber.

Millions of feet of lumber are annually shipped from Crescent City to ports in central and southern California. The well protected harbor is a welcome haven for those cruising up and down the coast.

There is good anchorage within its breakwaters with protection from both northwest and southerly winds. Fuel and supplies are available at this bay-fronting town, but no slips or moorings for pleasure craft.

Crescent City was first in the United States to use the Tetrapod in its breakwater construction. (Santa Cruz Harbor has since used these forms in their jetties.) These Tetrapods are concrete forms, molded in the approximate shape of a huge jackstone, weighing 25 tons each and standing 11 feet high. When in use on the seaward breakwater slopes, their irregular masses become firmly interlocked with each successive surge of a storm-driven sea, and provide far more security than would the same weight in stone. Although Crescent City suffered major damage from seismic floods resulting from the 1964 Alaska earthquake, such destruction as occurred here was estimated to be far less than it would have been without these unusually strong breakwaters.

St. George Reef, extending 6½ miles northwest of Point

Entrance to Rogue River, Oregon, has a 13-foot-deep channel, 300 feet wide between jetties. Passenger traffic (small-boat sportfishing fleet) in 1963 averaged nearly 38,000, attesting to the popularity of this prime fishing area for both ocean or fresh-water fish.

George, is well marked on its most seaward rock with a navigational light and a diaphone. When abeam this light, a more northerly course can be taken up the coast to Port Orford, Oregon, a span of some 55 miles. Well protected from the northwest by Cape Blanco, Port Orford provides good anchorage from all but southerly winds, and fuel and supplies are available at their village. This community is an export source of famed Port Orford yellow cedar, and great stands of these giant evergreens line the mountain slopes surrounding the anchorage, adding their spicy aroma to the cold salt air of the sea.

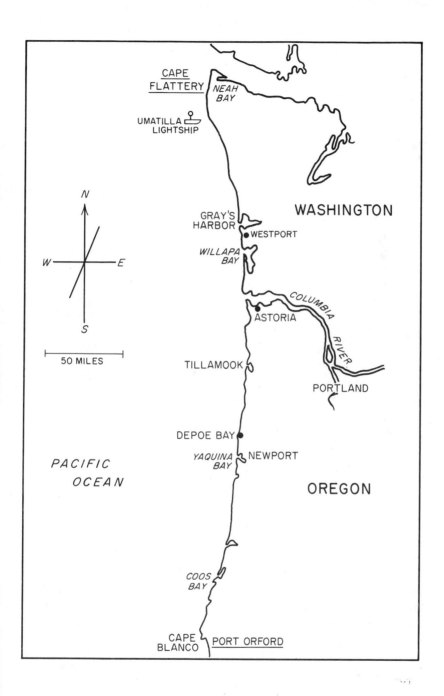

CHAPTER 7

Port Orford to Cape Flattery

Along the Oregon and Washington coasts there are a dozen major rivers pouring billions of gallons of pure mountain water into the Pacific. Though some of this water is wasted insofar as its primary purpose is concerned, the river mouths are welcomed by fishermen all up and down the shoreline. Fishing skiffs and small outboards use most of these exits to the ocean in all but stormy weather. They have been doing so since Indian times and most likely will continue to for years to come. But just because they *are* used at one time or another by a certain type of boat, it does not mean they should all be considered harbors of refuge for the ocean-cruising vessel. For this reason we will mention in this chapter only those ports which are better endowed with protection, and have easy access for the off-shore cruiser who may not have "local knowledge," a pertinent phrase used wisely in Pacific Coast Pilot and other marine guide books.

From Cape Blanco it is only 35 miles north to Coos Bay, the major deep-water harbor between San Francisco and the Columbia River. Coos Bay is home port to a variety of enterprises, lumber rating foremost, and sport and commercial fishing running a close second. Charleston pleasure-boat basin is situated just inside the southern jetty, affording all manner of marina facilities and charter fishing boats. Salmon, striped bass, tuna and shad are some of the more prolific ocean fish in the area. Oysters, clams and crabs are also to be had in abundance along Coos Bay's shoreline.

Inland, within the Port area, State parks and picnic grounds are plentiful for those who would tarry ashore to explore the scenic hinterland of wild fern, huckleberry, azalea and rhododendron. This is a land of rain and sudden sunshine, which combine with the area's mild year-round climate to extract the ultimate of richness in nature's verdure. One of the rare hard

Looking seaward over breakwatered entrance to Coos Bay, Oregon. Charleston Small Boat Basin has recently been enlarged to accommodate the growing fleet of sport and commercial fishing boats. Coos Bay is noted for sportfishing with salmon, striped bass and shad runs predominating in the ocean, and clams, Dungeness crab and oysters closer to shore.

woods indigenous to this coastal region is the golden, multi-whorled myrtlewood, from which novelties, furniture and gun stocks are fashioned and polished to mirror finish.

Cruising further north and after passing the river mouths of the Umpqua, Suislaw and the Alsea, we arrive at Yaquina Bay and Newport, Oregon. After the usual proper timing of a bar entrance into Yaquina Bay, the visiting boat will find good facilities, for either overnight or extended stay at Newport. This is another fisherman's heaven, with its ocean fishing augmented here by trout and steelhead angling along the Yaquina River, which is navigable up to 20 miles inland from the Bay. As elsewhere on the Oregon coast, State parks and camping sites are plentiful within a short range of the Bay. Some of these are situated along the forested river banks and others lie adjacent to the long expanses of duned, sand beaches on the ocean front. For the beachcomber-hiker, a rewarding stroll may be taken along the strand from Newport, 3 miles north to Agate Beach and Yaquina Head. Whether one returns heavily laden with agates, seashells, clams and crabs or with merely a driftwood walking stick, his body will benefit from the exercise and his spirit will be eased by such a peaceful sojourn.

Moving on north, past aptly named Cape Foulweather to a point about 9 miles beyond Yaquina Head, we approach a nar-

Controversial *Depoe Bay* on the Oregon coast, offers inner sanctuary to the daring coastal cruisers who may choose to negotiate its challenging entrance.

row corridor through the coastline's cliffs which leads into tiny Depoe Bay. The whole aspect is that of a doll-sized "sometimes" harbor. Despite its miniscule size, the presence of this little cove has engendered giant-sized arguments as to the advisability of its use by offshore cruising vessels. On the pro side of the question, it may be said that it can be negotiated by boats of up to 60 or 70 feet in length and less than 7-foot draft, *provided* that these vessels can safely clear Depoe bridge which spans its entrance. The bridge has a clearance of 50 feet from mean high water and is flood-lighted at night. There is much more that might be said *against* the use of Depoe as a harbor of refuge, but we prefer to let the matter rest with other published guides, such as Frank Morris' *Coastal Harbors of Oregon and Washington* and *Pacific Coast Pilot,* or with those skippers who have negotiated this controversial Depoe Bay more often than we have. Certainly the type of boat under consideration, the proficiency of its pilot, and the weather situation at time of a proposed entry will have much to do with such a decision. There are supplies and fuel available

Tillamook Bay and bar, North Jetty, 50 miles south of the mouth of the Columbia River. Channel depths start at 18 feet at ocean entrance, diminishing to a depth of 12 feet at the small-boat basin of Garibaldi.

inside "the hole," as it is referred to by local users of Depoe Bay.

The next major harbor to the north of Depoe is Tillamook Bay, 5 miles northward of Cape Meares Light. The channel entrance to this harbor averages 20 feet deep at the bar and is therefore little used by deep-sea vessels. Log rafts are towed or barged out of Tillamook Bay but it is used primarily by the commercial fishing fleet and pleasure boats. Supplies and fuel are available at the small boat basin in Garibaldi, which lies on the north shore of Tillamook Bay. Visitors are welcome to tour Tillamook's famous cheese factories, and there are canneries which will process a fish catch should the angler care to have his salmon or other marine take canned.

Beacon Rock, on the north bank of the Columbia River, is an ancient monolith, the core of a volcano. A Washington State Park with 4025 acres is located directly north of this 872-foot rock. A winding stairway takes you to the top. A boat moorage is in the Columbia River directly below.

From this point north to the Columbia River, shoreside scenery is one of scenic contrasts. Densely wooded heads or capes extend to seaward, curving down to meet white beaches with their row on row of tumbling breakers. Windswept evergreens crown the heights of sand dunes until the dunes give way to more jagged rocky points, scalloped off to infinity. This section of the coastline from Tillamook Bay to a point some 30 miles north, comprises the recreational beach area of the Oregon coast. From Rockaway Beach at the southern end up to Seaside and Gearhart Beach beyond Tillamook Head—all are focal points for summer visitors.

There is probably no other major port on the Pacific Coast that is as well charted and detailed as is the Columbia River's entrance. The bar can become too rough to cross at times, but with clear, mild weather and at flood tide, even the smallest craft should have no difficulty in negotiating its corridor of well-marked buoys and navigational aids. From Astoria and Warrenton, the first cities inside the river mouth, the Columbia continues inland for many hundreds of miles. Together with its many tributaries to the east, north and south, the extent of opportunities it affords for pleasure boatsmen to enjoy their craft in protected waters is far too vast for description here. From a point near Astoria, both fresh water and ocean fishing are readily available. Further inland, along the Columbia and its main tributary, the Willamette, water pleasures turn to swimming, water skiing, fast boat racing or simply scenic cruising or sailing. Months on end could be spent in these waterways where one river joins another to create a water path reaching beyond the State of Oregon and into Washington and Idaho. Nearly all river marinas have launching ramps as well as small boats for charter or hourly hire, and picnicking and camping sites are only a few miles apart.

Cape Disappointment marks the northerly point of land at Columbia River's entrance. The River itself is a border division between Oregon and Washington. Twenty-five miles beyond Cape Disappointment is the first of Washington's two coastal harbors. This is Willapa Bay, previously known as Shoalwater Bay, because it is just that. The usual ocean fishing is engaged in outside the harbor while inside, emphasis is on the succulent Willapa oyster, Dungeness crabs and clams. Willapa's entrance bar is continually shifting, and special care must be used in negotiating the fluctuating depths of this channel. Tokeland, 8 miles

in from the bar, is the center of sport-fishing activity where supplies, motels and charter fishing boats await their many customers.

As we have mentioned earlier, most of our trips to the northwest have been made either non-stop from Los Angeles to Cape
Flattery, or with relatively few overnight stops at harbors along
the northern part of the coast. With our ship's ample fuel supply
this could be done with relative ease, and it avoided our having
to cross the bar entrances to Oregon and Washington harbors.
The one exception to this pattern happened a few years ago
when we found ourselves with little choice but to cross the bar
into Gray's Harbor, approximately 25 miles northward of Willapa Bay—worse yet, having to cross in the maelstrom of an
ebbing tide.

It was in the middle of a night, when we were about 30 miles
offshore and some 40 miles northwest of Gray's Harbor, that our
ship took one particularly hard roll which dislodged the lead
tray containing our 2000 pounds of batteries. One end of the
tray was canted at a precarious angle resting against an engine,

Gray's Harbor, Washington, is home to one of the State's largest fishing
fleets. Salmon is the major catch during all but winter months, at which time
crab fishers bring in thousands of pounds of the Pacific's finest shellfish, the
Dungeness Crab.

and the other was caught temporarily on a CO_2 tank. The major threat was loss of power for radio, radar, pumps and other auxiliaries if the batteries should further tip and lose their acid, or if the now-taut 110-volt power cables should be torn loose by further movement.

There were just three of us aboard, Jack and I, and our son Gordon. We had work to do and some decisions to make in a hurry. Small-craft warnings were displayed north to Cape Flattery and our present heading of 350 degrees kept us in a mean quartering sea. Our best solution appeared to turn downwind and head for Gray's Harbor for repairs. Jack and Gordon went to work in the engineroom with two-by-fours and nails, shoring up the battery tray as best they could with meager supplies. Meanwhile I took the wheel and tried to steer as smooth a course as possible in the stormy, cresting seas.

As we yawed along in the early morning hours, we discussed the cause of our battery shift. There had been, we knew, about $\frac{1}{4}$ inch of space between the batteries and their containing tray. Inertia from our heavy roll had started the movement which generated enough force to tear loose the wooden bulkhead supports—supports which were never intended to have strength for such a sudden thrust.

Dawn came, raw and gray, all the more unpleasant for us with our lack of sleep, and the tension of the preceding hours. Earlier we had called Coast Guard explaining our predicament and asking them to lead us through the devious channel to Westport. When we met them outside the harbor, it was apparent that they would have preferred us to stay outside another six hours until change of tide; but we felt our temporary shoring in the engineroom would probably not withstand such an interval of waiting and circling outside the bar.

"We'll go in now," Jack told their skipper. "All right," he replied tersely. "Follow me in, but if you lose your radio, strike your colors."

Tired as we were, we laughed at that last message. If we did lose our radio power it would likely mean we had lost everything aboard ship at the same time in one big roll. Just who, I asked, is going to dash sixty feet aft to haul down Old Glory?

Although the Coast Guard cutter was a 125-foot ship and she stayed about 300 yards ahead of us on our wild ride across the bar, its mast often disappeared completely from our sight in those tremendous seas. Seas that came up from everywhere and smashed against themselves in indescribable fury! It was no wonder to us that more people and ships have been lost at Gray's Harbor than have been at any other Pacific coast port. After twenty minutes of back-breaking work at the wheel for Jack (most of the time it meant full rudder from block to block) we slewed and wallowed our way into somewhat calmer waters. Part of the time the marker buoys were out of sight behind towering seas. We were doubly glad to have a leader.

A carpenter in Westport spent most of the day helping us put our engineroom back in order. It took house-moving jacks to lift the battery tray back into position. And when we headed out of Gray's Harbor channel on the following morning, their bar was smooth as a lake. It was hard to realize this was the same bar

Neah Bay's entrance, looking northward across Strait of Juan de Fuca toward Vancouver Island. The Coast Guard Station is in foreground; anchorage to west of their dock.

that for us had almost turned out to be the one in the well-known hymn.

Another 80 miles northwest of Gray's Harbor north jetty light, Umatilla Light Ship tugs at her moorings. This we keep to starboard, and on a more northerly heading point toward Cape Flattery, 16 miles beyond. The Cape marks the end of the line for Washington's rugged coastline, and fittingly sums up the State's whole coastal aspect in one great exclamation point. High on Waatch Hill stands one of the Pacific's largest radar Early Warning installations. Below, along the wild and rocky shoreline, the sea thunders its eternal rage against a lonely beach where drift logs lie like scattered monstrous matchsticks, and sea birds fly screaming down the wind-torn sky.

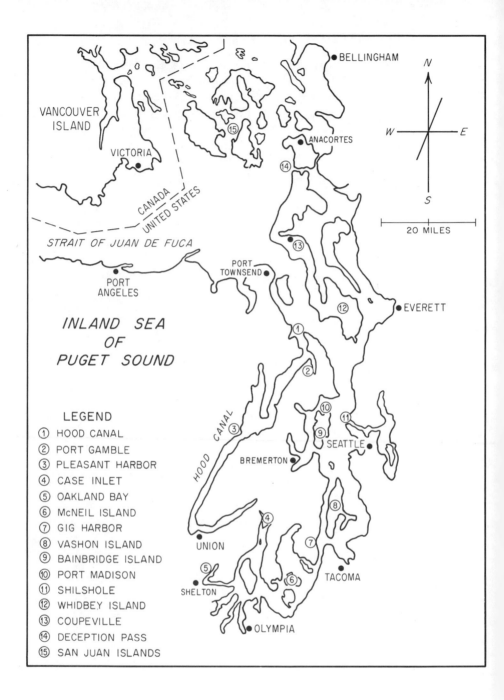

N

W   E

S

20 MILES

BELLINGHAM

VANCOUVER
ISLAND

VICTORIA

ANACORTES

⑮

⑭

CANADA
UNITED STATES

STRAIT OF JUAN DE FUCA

⑬

PORT
TOWNSEND

PORT
ANGELES

EVERETT

⑫

INLAND SEA
OF
PUGET SOUND

①

②

⑩

⑪

LEGEND

① HOOD CANAL
② PORT GAMBLE
③ PLEASANT HARBOR
④ CASE INLET
⑤ OAKLAND BAY
⑥ McNEIL ISLAND
⑦ GIG HARBOR
⑧ VASHON ISLAND
⑨ BAINBRIDGE ISLAND
⑩ PORT MADISON
⑪ SHILSHOLE
⑫ WHIDBEY ISLAND
⑬ COUPEVILLE
⑭ DECEPTION PASS
⑮ SAN JUAN ISLANDS

HOOD CANAL

③

⑨

SEATTLE

BREMERTON

⑧

④

⑦

UNION

⑤

⑥

TACOMA

SHELTON

OLYMPIA

CHAPTER 8

The Inland Sea of Puget Sound

Little did Senor Juan de Fuca realize, back in 1590, that his orders from the Viceroy of Spanish Mexico to find the Northwest Passage would someday be recounted in a cruising guide to the Pacific Coast. But no guide to the Inland Sea of Puget Sound would be complete without a brief review of the claims and counterclaims of the discovery of the Northwest Passage, which was reported by Juan de Fuca to have had its western terminus in the Strait that now bears his name.

The Spanish, English and Dutch sent expedition after expedition to find the mythical Northwest Passage that would shorten their trade routes to the Orient by giving passage from the Atlantic Coast to the Pacific. It was in 1592 that Juan de Fuca reported having sailed 20 days eastward from Cape Flattery (although it was not so-named until 180 years later) and claimed that he had reached the Atlantic Ocean through the new passage.

Despite Juan de Fuca's positive statements (which even named the approximate latitude of the entrance to the passage) Capt. James Cook from England stated in his log as late as 1772: "It is in this very latitude where we now are that geographers have placed the pretended Strait of Juan de Fuca. But we saw nothing like it, nor is there the least probability that any such thing existed." Cook even sailed past the entrance to the Strait, and the theoretical entrance to the Northwest Passage, without observing it. He did name the bluff at its entrance "Cape Flattery."

It was not until 1792 that Capt. George Vancouver, also from England, with two small ships, the *Discovery* and the *Chatham*, finally put world geographers straight on the Northwest Passage. Among the 145 officers and men making up the crews of the two ships were Capt. Joseph Whidbey and Lt. Peter Puget. Their names and others of the British Admiralty were appropriately given to discoveries made by Capt. Vancouver. They entered the

157

Strait of Juan de Fuca in April of that year, and in six months charted the waters of Puget Sound and the Strait of Georgia. They also proved that Vancouver Island, later named after Capt. Vancouver, was not a part of the mainland. Every possible inlet reaching eastward was explored, and Vancouver rightfully concluded that the Northwest Passage was a myth that had existed for nearly two hundred years.

In early June of 1792 Capt. Vancouver wrote the first account of northwest boat-racing activities, by reporting the canoe races of the Indians. In an area now named Coupeville, on the eastern shores of Whidbey Island, his survey party came on friendly tribes of Indians who tested the strength of their youth in racing hand-carved, cedar-log canoes—not small dugouts, but heavy 45- to 50-foot canoes, with crews of eight handling brightly painted paddles. Today those same Indian canoe races are staged annually and draw hundreds of yachtsmen to watch them, from all parts of Puget Sound.

Notwithstanding the high northerly latitude of this area, it is blessed with a mild climate. Average winter temperature is 41 degrees and the summer 63 degrees, thanks to the Japanese current which brings warmth to an area that would otherwise be as cold as the northeastern tip of the States.

A single statement can sum up the magnitude of the Puget Sound cruising region: "Here a boatowner could live to be a hundred years old and never anchor twice in the same cove." There is an estimated 20,000 miles of shoreline, with good anchorages never more than a few miles apart. With few exceptions, provisions and fuel are obtainable without going more than 25 miles. In recent years the State of Washington has taken an active and commendable step in building small-boat mooring facilities at scores of water-recreational areas including overnight camping sites ashore for those who are cruising in open boats. It is the farsightedness of the State, Counties and communities of Washington that has helped spur the tremendous increase in use of the 2000 square miles of inland waters.

From the standpoint of the type of craft that is suitable for Northwest cruising, the answer is literally "anything that floats and is seaworthy." Outboard runabouts and cruisers are proving increasingly popular, and because of the many overnight shoreside facilities, extended trips in outboard powered boats are routine. On the other hand, deep-draft sail and power boats have no problem because the entire area from lower Puget Sound to

All Seattle boats dress in their best for Opening Day parades. Here the fleet lines up to move from Portage Bay through Montlake Cut into Lake Washington.

Alaska is "deep water." While the weather from June to October is mild, there are times when foul-weather gear is desirable. For this reason there are fewer of the flying-bridge type of cruisers in the Northwest than in other areas of the Pacific Coast. This is also why wood- or oil-burning galley ranges are used to provide year-around warmth on many sail and power boats.

Fishing, crabbing, oyster plucking and clam digging are more popular extracurricular activities than is swimming or water skiing. Average water temperatures are in the mid-50's or low 60's, except in isolated or protected areas.

While there are hundreds of sailing enthusiasts in Northwest waters, the area is better suited to power boats. A glance at one of the accompanying charts shows the reason: there are not too many long reaches of open water. Another deterrent to a larger sailing fleet are the tides and resulting currents, reaching 3 to 7 knots in some of the most picturesque passages, such as Admiralty Inlet, which is between Whidbey Island and the mainland to the west, or in Saratoga Passage between Whidbey Island and the mainland to the east. The result is an increasing number of motor sailers finding popularity in these waters, as contrasted to the deep-water sailing types.

There are two main cruising areas between Port Townsend at the entrance to Puget Sound and the southern extremity of the "Inland Sea." The easternmost of the two has on its shores Olympia (the State Capitol), Tacoma, Seattle, Bremerton, Everett, Anacortes and Bellingham; the western area in Hood Canal, with its opening near Port Townsend. Misnamed a "canal" by Capt. Vancouver, the name has stuck with this 55-mile-long fiord which cuts deeply into the Olympic Peninsula. There are no com-

Puget Sound is not always smooth, as is obvious here during annual Heavy-weather Race.

munities of size on the Canal, although scores of summer resorts and a number of lumber mill villages are along the shores to remind those cruising that they are not a million miles from civilization.

Starting down the Canal on a southwesterly heading from Foulweather Bluff, the first stop is usually at Hood Point for a sack of the oysters which abound the rocky beach during low tide. Two miles farther on the left is the 100-yard-wide entrance to Port Gamble, where supplies of all kinds can be obtained from the lumbermill-operated fuel docks and store. A land-locked harbor, it is a frequent haven for those not wanting to make the run to the Canal's southern end. Just past the entrance to Port Gamble is the world's longest floating bridge spanning a salt-water channel. Between Port Gamble and the south end of the Canal are harbors or coves that can easily go unnoticed because of their small openings along the Canal. Aptly-named Pleasant Harbor is one of them, with a narrow mouth that opens into a forest-lined cove of serenity. At low tide, boats drawing more than 4 feet should not enter the harbor, although once inside, there is plenty of water. Twenty miles farther south, where the Canal takes a sharp turn to the northeast, is one of the larger Indian Reservations and nearby, the village of Union, where fuel and supplies are available.

Less than 2 miles of land separates Lynch Cove at the end of the Canal from Case Inlet on the Olympia side of Puget Sound. No doubt Capt. Vancouver failed to reach this point in his early surveys and assumed the two bodies of water were connected.

Within a 15-mile radius of Olympia are a half-dozen arms, inlets or passages that are a deterrent to sailing enthusiasts, but a cruising paradise to the power-boat owners. Typical is Hammersley Inlet, which terminates in Oakland Bay. In a distance of 10 miles through this forest-lined waterway there are at least 14 changes of direction as the Inlet unwinds on its way past the lumbertown of Shelton. And to cover the 22 miles, as the seagulls fly, between Olympia and Tacoma, there are a dozen different routes that can be taken around scores of small islands. The best-known island along this part of the Sound is McNeil (also known as the "resort," because of its Federal Prison), which commands a millionaire's view of the Sound and the majestic Olympic and Cascade mountain ranges.

Tacoma is approached from the lower Sound through The Narrows—well named because of towering cliffs close on each

Hale Passage, between Tacoma and Olympia, Washington, in southern Puget Sound.

other. Here currents reach velocities up to 6 knots as they are compressed through the channel. Over The Narrows is one of the largest suspension bridges in the country, built a few years ago after the original one was blown down during a terrific winter storm. Tacoma Yacht Club is located 2 miles southeast of Pt. Defiance—the northern extremity of The Narrows, in a landlocked harbor, only a few minutes' drive from Tacoma's residential area. Fortunate are these residents in that they can cruise either to the north toward Seattle or toward Olympia to the south, with hundreds of miles of shoreline and scores of coves in which to anchor between their club and the two cities.

The north end of The Narrows has on its west bank the well-known community of Gig Harbor, made famous by the commercial fishing boats that ply Pacific waters, a distinctive type of which is built here. Populated mainly by families of Scandinavian and Spanish descent, Gig Harbor is a colorful and hospitable rendezvous for northwest cruising enthusiasts.

Between Tacoma and Seattle is 10-mile-long Vashon Island, which is connected by a sandspit to Moury Island. At Portage Spit there is usually held each year the historic Indian Clam Bake. While the procedure seems simple, it takes the native Indians to get the right touch, first in digging an immense basin in the sand, lining it with rocks, and building the driftwood fire (which burns for a day to heat the rocks); then filling of the basin with alternate layers of seaweed, clams, chicken and salmon, topped by a blanket of seaweed. Nearby are five-gallon cans of clams, steaming in broth unequaled even by the French Bordelaise. In the bay will be anchored all types of boats from all parts of the Sound and around beach fires will be gathered the owners

Gig Harbor, looking eastward across The Narrows toward Tacoma.

and their guests for an Indian feast that can be equalled only by similar ones.

Ten miles to the north of Portage one finds Seattle to the east, and the entrance channels to Bremerton to the west. Winding between the south end of Bainbridge Island and the mainland is the channel which leads to Sinclair Inlet, on which Bremerton is situated and where the Puget Sound Navy Yard is the principal activity.

Another of Puget Sound's favorite clam-digging areas is Hidden Harbor behind Bremerton, reached through Washington Narrows which connects Dyes Inlet and Sinclair Inlet. Completely landlocked, Hidden Harbor is a bowl of water garnished with towering evergreen trees that come down to the sand beach, and at low tide yield never-ending supplies of butter clams.

Cruising toward the northern end of Bainbridge Island brings one to Port Madison. It has become a year-around residential area for many who have in their front yards a pier or float for their boats, which they use to commute to Seattle. This is also the site of Seattle Yacht Club's "Fo'castle," a facility which many yacht clubs would be proud to call their headquarters. Floats are provided for visiting boats and a roaring cordwood fire is usually burning in a massive fireplace in the lounge. Although only ¼ mile wide by a mile in length, Port Madison will frequently have 40 to 50 boats anchored in it on weekends, since it is only an hour's cruise from Shilshole Bay and the Locks at Seattle.

It is through these Locks that thousands of pleasure and commercial boats pass each season from Lakes Union and Washington, around which Seattle is built. During peak traffic hours, the main lock (the largest on the North American continent) will have hundreds of small boats in it on their way to or from the Sound. Within the last few years a breakwater and slip facilities for nearly 2000 boats has been completed at Shilshole Bay, on the Sound side. This is directly to the north of the entrance to the Locks, and is a boon to Seattle boat owners who prefer not to face the weekend bottleneck at the Locks. Excellent restaurants are here, as well as supplies and fuel. It is operated by the Seattle Port Commission and is an oustanding example of a port-authority-operated marina.

Before we leave Seattle, it should be noted that during mid winter and spring, while Pacific coast boatsmen are cruising,

A portion of the Port of Seattle's Shilshole Bay Yacht Anchorage on Puget Sound.

racing and sailing, a group of its civic leaders spends week after week planning and working on the annual Seafair celebration. Founded some years ago, this has become a water carnival, an aquatic festival, a period of worship (by boat owners to King Neptune). Spanning from ten days to two weeks during August, the Seattle Seafair has had on its program the outboard championship races, the Gold Cup unlimited hydroplane races, national water-skiing competitions, Pacific Coast championship inboard races for all classes, sailing events, and even the Aquacade swimming pageant. For the latter, the city built on Green Lake a stadium seating 40,000 persons on three sides of a special pool, backed by a stage.

Cruising northward from Seattle invariably takes one to San Juan Islands, either up the east or westward sides of Whidbey Island. The westward side, through Admiralty Inlet, is the main steamer lane, passing the entrance to Hood Canal and finally past Port Townsend. The only hazards are the thousands of weekend fishermen in the waters during the salmon-fishing season.

Going toward the San Juans via Saratoga Passage on the eastern side of Whidbey Island is by far the most scenic route. There are innumerable harbors or anchoring spots along the Island; excellent clam-digging beaches and the historic Indian village of Coupeville. The climax of this route is Deception Pass, through which tides will pour or empty at velocities of up to 8 knots. Just east of the Pass and on Whidbey Island is Coronet

Looking west through Deception Pass, during slack water.

Bay, a development of the State Parks and Recreation Commission, with docks, floats, camping grounds, showers and barbecue pits. It is a favorite layover harbor for those waiting for slack water. A similar facility is at the western entrance to the Pass.

After passing through Deception Pass, heading westerly, the San Juan Archipelago of some 172 islands come into view—all spaced within a rectangular area measuring 15 miles by 20 miles.

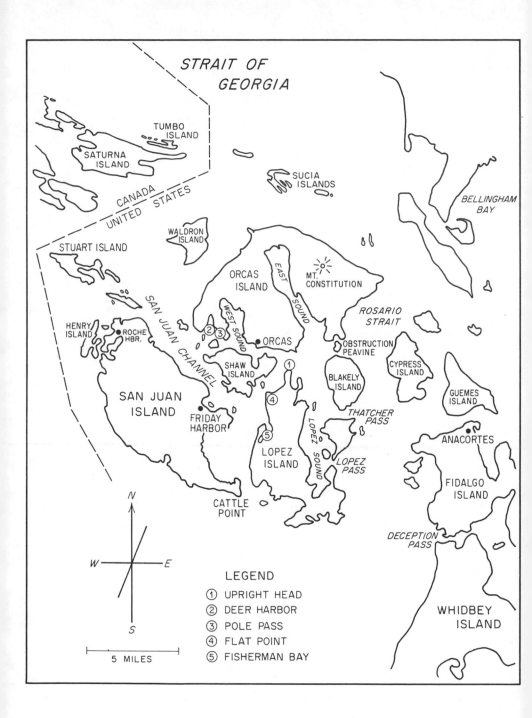

STRAIT OF GEORGIA

TUMBO ISLAND

SATURNA ISLAND

CANADA
UNITED STATES

SUCIA ISLANDS

BELLINGHAM BAY

WALDRON ISLAND

STUART ISLAND

ORCAS ISLAND

MT. CONSTITUTION

EAST SOUND

ROSARIO STRAIT

HENRY ISLAND

ROCHE HBR.

SAN JUAN CHANNEL

WEST SOUND

② ③

ORCAS

OBSTRUCTION PEAVINE

CYPRESS ISLAND

SHAW ISLAND

①

BLAKELY ISLAND

GUEMES ISLAND

SAN JUAN ISLAND

④

THATCHER PASS

ANACORTES

FRIDAY HARBOR

⑤

LOPEZ SOUND

LOPEZ PASS

LOPEZ ISLAND

FIDALGO ISLAND

CATTLE POINT

DECEPTION PASS

N

W —— E

S

WHIDBEY ISLAND

LEGEND
① UPRIGHT HEAD
② DEER HARBOR
③ POLE PASS
④ FLAT POINT
⑤ FISHERMAN BAY

5 MILES

CHAPTER 9

The San Juan Archipelago

Leaving Deception Pass on our cruise among the San Juan Islands, we have the choice of six passages into the lake-smooth waters of the archipelago. Four of these are from Rosario Strait on the eastern side of the Islands; they are most generally used when approaching the Islands from Deception Pass (or Anacortes and Bellingham, which are to the north of the Pass) because the distances are shorter.

If we approach the Islands from the Strait of Juan de Fuca or Puget Sound we would use Middle Channel, past Cattle Point on the southern tip of San Juan Island; or if returning southbound from British Columbia, we would use the northwestern portion of San Juan Channel.

Even though the *Coast Pilot* makes the statement that Lopez Pass, between Lopez and Decatur Islands, "is little used . . . and very narrow" it must be remembered that this is written primarily for the benefit of ocean-going vessel masters, and not for the average small-boat owner. With 9 to 12 fathoms of water through the passage, and deep water up to the steep shores of the Islands, Lopez Pass is free of hazards and the closest one to Deception Pass. In fact, the 8-mile passage across Rosario Strait from Deception can provide far more excitement if it is made during ebb tide with a strong afternoon breeze from the west.

Alternate access to the 15-mile-long Lopez and East Sounds from Rosario Strait is through the half-mile-wide Thatcher Pass, which is about 3 miles to the north of Lopez Pass; or through either Obstruction or Peavine Passes, another 5 miles north of Thatcher. All lead to the landlocked, island-studded waters of Lopez Sound and East Sound, formed by Lopez, Decatur, Blakely and Orcas Islands. These are oft referred to as the eastern part of the San Juans, as contrasted to San Juan, Henry, Stuart and Waldron Islands, which make up the western part of the archi-

169

Looking westward, Lopez Pass, San Juan Islands. Ram Island, left center.

pelago. Standing to the north of Orcas Island are the jewel-like Sucia Islands, with their deep indentations and protected anchorages.

Once within the Lopez and East Sounds, roughly from ½ mile to 2 miles wide and 15 miles north-south, there are virtually countless anchoring areas. Largest of the Islands that give protection to these waters is Orcas, with its 2454-foot-high Mt. Constitution dominating the scene. For those with long legs (and the constitution) to climb Mt. Constitution it is a rewarding outing, because it provides a bird's-eye view of the entire group of islands, the mainland of Washington to the east, Vancouver Island to the west, the Canadian Strait of Georgia to the north and Puget Sound to the south.

A number of small communities are on these two Sounds, and cruising supplies are readily available. Most have docks for the ferries that are the principal links with the mainland to the east, and to the other communities in the San Juan group. Olga, Rosario and Eastsound have particularly good facilities for visiting boats, with floats, supplies and at Eastsound an airstrip for plane-commuting back to the mainland or to the other airstrips on nearby islands.

Heading westward between Upright Head on the northwestern tip of Lopez Island and the southern tip of a portion of Orcas Island, we have the choice of passing Shaw Island through the northerly passages, or turning southwest for the more direct route to Friday Harbor on San Juan Island.

Staying on the northerly of the two passages takes us past the community of Orcas and into West Sound which is a 3-mile-long indentation into Orcas Island. Good dockage is available at the small community of Westsound, and anchorage can be taken practically anywhere within the Sound. Going toward Deer Harbor from West Sound can sometimes present a thrill while in Pole Pass. It is 75 yards wide at its narrowest point, and passage through it should be timed for slack or near-slack water, to avoid currents that can reach 8 knots at the height of their ebb or flood. Deer Harbor is the westernmost of the secluded ones on Orcas Island, and only about 7 miles from the archipelago's metropolis of Friday Harbor.

Had we turned southwest from Upright Head on Lopez Island, we would have passed Flat Point, one of the area's greatest salmon-fishing spots, enroute to the landlocked Fisherman Bay. Frequently it is overlooked or passed by without realizing that the S-shaped channel leads into the resort community of Lopez. Completely protected from all winds, Fisherman Bay has an excellent holding bottom or dockage for visiting boats, supplies, and a restaurant at the shore end of the pier with a view towards the west and San Juan Island that is breath-taking.

Only about 4 miles westerly of Lopez is the county seat of Friday Harbor, on the easterly shores of San Juan Island. Separating Lopez and San Juan Islands is the San Juan Channel, which is one of the three principal passages between Puget Sound and British Columbia waters to the north (the other two being on the eastern and western sides of the archipelago). The Channel is about 13 miles long and varies in width from $\frac{1}{2}$ to 3 miles, through which the ebb and flood tides set up currents that reach as high as 5 knots as they pass Cattle Point on the Puget Sound end of the Channel. Sailing through this Channel without the help of an auxiliary engine is frustrating, and unless one is going with the current it can be slow and exasperating.

Friday Harbor is a quaint mixture of a fishing village, summer resort, cannery town and shopping center. It is linked to the mainland with good ferry service the year around, and both charter and scheduled small-plane service. On the northern part

Beachcombing on Jones Island, about 5 miles north of Friday Harbor, is a relaxing weekend activity. This is one of the rare island beaches. Usually trees grow right to water's edge, with ample anchorage depths close to shore.

of the Harbor is a University of Washington oceanographic facility. It is the center of a prosperous agricultural district and the headquarters for a sizable fishing fleet. In contrast to the new and modern motel facilities, until recently one of the older hotels was still using knotted ropes from the second-story windows for fire escapes.

In the middle of the roughly one mile, semi-circular Harbor is heavily wooded Brown Island, with channels leading to Friday Harbor docks on either side of the Island. Waters here, as throughout the entire archipelago, are deep to within a few hundred yards of the shorelines. Anchorage in the harbor in 5 to 8 fathoms is frequently necessary when the city-maintained floats are filled with visiting craft. Friday Harbor is also a port of entry for those returning from Canadian waters, and during the sum-

Historic Roche Harbor, San Juan Islands.

mer months the yacht clubs in Puget Sound underwrite the over-
time charges that would otherwise be assessed for customs clearance during holidays and Sundays.

On the northwestern end of the roughly 15-mile-long San Juan
Island is a popular boating destination, Roche Harbor. We had
previously gone past it many times, enroute to Canadian waters,
until Frank Morris, coauthor of the *Marine Atlas of the Northwest,* urged us to visit his summer home a short distance from it.
We are glad that he did, because we found at Roche Harbor
floats to accommodate a large fleet of summer-resident boats, and
still ample room for visiting craft. Ashore there are supply stores;
the same small hotel with restaurant that once catered to the visiting businessmen and sailing ship captains who came to the
harbor in the early 1900's; and a giant-size barbecue pit that can

provide barbecued salmon and meat for hundreds of guests at one time.

A short walk through a tree- and shrub-lined trail is a stark reminder of Roche Harbor's early days. In the center of a forest clearing stands a circle of Grecian columns, surrounding an enormous cement table and cement chairs around the table. It is said that under the seat of each chair are the ashes of the family members. A close look at the total picture shows that one chair is missing, and the upper part of one column is unfinished. It is local lore that the elimination of the chair and part of the column represented the one "black sheep" of the family who was not entitled to join his family, even after death.

At the turn of the century Roche Harbor was a bustling community, producing millions of tons of high-quality lime that was shipped to the four corners of the world. Now all that remains of the lime quarries and mill are graying skeletons of buildings and boarded-up entrances to mining shafts. On the pier that once saw sailing vessels of many nations tied to it while loading their cargoes are now facilities for visiting boat owners, and the Roche Harbor Yacht Club.

Within a few minutes' outboarding in a dinghy to the west of Roche Harbor is Henry Island, with its picturesque King's Ransom Cove where, it is said, smugglers frequently took refuge from pursuers. Hardly a mile further through Mosquito Passage is the entrance to Westcott Bay, completely land-locked and with sand beaches around its perimeter. On a bite off Westcott Bay is the site of the old English Camp and blockhouse, remindful of the days of dispute between the English and United States over the boundary between the two countries.

Four miles northerly from Roche Harbor is Stuart Island, with its two fine harbors that provide quiet seclusion and perfect weather protection. Reid Harbor is on the south side of the Island, about a mile in length and ending at a broad, sloping beach that is ideal for clam-digging. On the north side is Prevost Harbor, where there is a dock and supplies can be obtained. Although less than $\frac{1}{4}$-mile-wide neck of land separates Reid and Prevost Harbors, to cruise from one to the other is a 4-mile trip through the narrow, but perfectly safe, John's Pass.

In contrast to the 3, 4 or 5 miles of cruising between such anchorages as Rosario, Olga, West Sound, Fisherman Bay, Friday Harbor, Roche Harbor, Reid and Prevost, each of which offers days of exploring in its immediate vicinity, the 12-mile run

Stuart Island, in the U.S. San Juan Island group, borders British Columbian territory.

from Stuart Island to Sucia Islands provides a distinct change of scene. Enroute on a northeasterly heading is Waldron Island, and like all the others in the San Juans, it is timbered nearly to the high-tide line. On its western shore is the community of Waldron, with a dock, supplies and shoreside facilities. If the weather is warm, the sand beaches by Waldron invite the swimming enthusiast. On its easterly shore is a small bite that provides good anchorage, and ashore are a few summer homes.

Our Sucia Islands destination is probably one of the most pleasant in the San Juan Island group. The State of Washington has provided floats, shoreside barbecue pits and camping facilities and there is ample room on both the east and west sides of the main, horseshoe-shaped Island to anchor without fear of swinging into another anchored boat. Echo Bay on the eastern side is a

Anchored in Reid Harbor, on Stuart Island in the San Juans of northern Puget Sound (a Washington State Marine Park).

mile-deep cut into the Island, with two narrow, wooded islets splitting the southern part of the Bay at its entrance. Deep water is on either side of the larger of the two islets, although most boats pass to the north of the larger of them. Fossil Bay is on the south side of the Islands, and although smaller in area than Echo Bay, it often has as many as 50 boats at the State floats or at anchor.

July, August and September are the prime months for San Juan Island cruising, both from a weather standpoint and for good salmon fishing, oyster plucking, clam digging or crab trapping. The "season" is purported to last five months, rather than three, but after a great many cruises into this territory aboard our *Monsoon* or *Monsoon II* we remain staunch supporters of the three summer months.

The ardent fisherman may not mind rain provided he comes in with his catch, and of that he may be assured regardless of weather. Of the many types of salmon caught in these waters, the King and Silvers are the main take for sportsfishermen, July and August being the best fishing months. The Blackmouth, a two-year immature King, is caught almost all year around. The

Boats moor in the quiet of Sucia Island, which lies directly north of Orcas Island, largest of the San Juan Archipelago in north Puget Sound.

Humpback, another fighter, is normally caught in the odd-numbered years and his run is short. Regardless of one's fishing luck, however, there is always a small harbor store within a few miles' cruising distance where one may buy his seafood, fresh from the water and awaiting the barbecue or frypan.

In the San Juan group of islands a decided change in weather and temperature is noticeable. It is warmer and dryer than the areas both north and south. The annual rainfall is less than half that of Seattle or Vancouver, B. C., which has led the area to be known as the "sunshine group" of islands, and by others as the "banana belt" of the northwest.

Appendix to Part II

Facilities and Supplies
Books and Charts
Permits for Offshore Islands
Electric/Electronic Equipment
Types of Boats suitable for Coastal Cruising
Table of Distances Between Harbors and Anchorages

FACILITIES AND SUPPLIES—CALIFORNIA, OREGON AND WASHINGTON

There are few harbors along the Pacific Coast that are not well able to serve the cruising boatman's needs of fuel, water, ice, mechanical and electronic supplies or repairs, stores and provisions. The few that do not are the anchorages under the lees of headlands, which are yet to be developed as breakwatered anchorages. Typical of the latter are Coxo Anchorage, the harbors on the islands to seaward of Santa Barbara, San Simeon and Shelter-Cove along the California coastline.

The thousands of commercial fishing vessels, and the growing number of pleasure craft that operate along the coast have created a demand for supplies and services that leaves little to be desired. Ship-to-shore communications, through the public correspondence stations, permit almost continuous contact with those ashore. Such stations are located at San Pedro, San Francisco, Eureka, Astoria and Seattle, and the majority of them have two or more channels to handle the traffic. Weather reports are broadcast by these stations, as well as by the Coast Guard. Continuous ESSA VHF reports are broadcast in the Los Angeles and San Francisco areas.

178

BOOKS AND CHARTS

Coast Pilot published by U. S. Coast & Geodetic Survey; Vol. 7 covers California, Oregon, Washington and Hawaii.

Boating & Fishing Almanac by William Berssen (Box 344, Venice, Calif.) covers Southern California ocean and inland waters.

How to Fish The Pacific Coast by Raymond Cannon (Lane Publishing Co., Menlo Park, Calif.).

Marine Atlas by Frank Morris and Willis R. Heath (P.B.I. Co., Box 54, Seattle, Wash.) Volume I includes especially drawn charts with courses and distances between Olympia, Wash. and Port Hardy, Vancouver Island, B.C., and many detailed chartlets of harbors, air photos and information on facilities available to those cruising the region.

Coastal Harbors of Oregon and Washington by Frank Morris and Willis R. Heath (P. B. I. Co., Box 54, Seattle, Wash.).

Sea Cruising Handbook published by Miller Freeman Publications, Inc., 500 Howard Street, San Francisco, Calif.

Northern California Boating Atlas published by Sunset Magazine. (Lane Publishing Co., Menlo Park, California.)

Sea Guide, by Leland R. Lewis and Peter E. Ebling, published by George Rice & Sons, Los Angeles, Calif. Covers So. Calif.

Northwest Passages by Bruce Calhoun (Miller Freeman Publications, Inc., 500 Howard St., San Francisco, Calif.)

Charts published by the U. S. Coast & Geodetic Survey are available through local agents in practically every harbor. Recently C & G S have developed *Small Craft Charts,* for such areas as Los Angeles–Long Beach, the San Francisco–San Pablo Bay and parts of Puget Sound. These have a great amount of detailed information on them, including tabulations of local facilities that are available, courses and distances. In addition, the major oil companies have cruising charts for the more popular areas, with varying amounts of local information to augment the charts. Besides the maritime charts, complete sets of aeronautical charts are helpful because they show the locations and frequencies of many low-frequency beacons, broadcast stations and VOR ranges that are not shown on all maritime charts.

PERMITS FOR OFFSHORE ISLANDS

Permits to go ashore on the western end of Santa Cruz Island may be obtained by mail: Santa Cruz Island Company, 615 S. Flower St., Los Angeles, Calif. Price: $20 per year, or $5.00 for any 30 consecutive days.

A shoregoing permit for this island's eastern portion (from Coche Point on the north, around the eastern end to Sandstone Point, including Potato Bay, Scorpion, Smugglers' and Yellowbanks Coves) may be obtained by writing: Mr. Pier Gherini, 230 La Arcada Blvd., Santa Barbara, or Mr. Francis Gherini, 162 South "A" St., Oxnard, Calif. This permit is without charge.

Pyramid Cove, on San Clemente Island's southeastern end may be used for anchoring when Naval exercises are not being conducted. No shoregoing is permissible in this restricted area.

ELECTRIC/ELECTRONIC EQUIPMENT

There are many cruising areas on the Pacific Coast where the ability to anchor (instead of tying to a dock or slip, or mooring on a buoy) adds greatly to the pleasure of the cruise. This encourages the use of an electric-power anchor windlass and ample chain. Radio-navigation aids are closely spaced along the entire coast, and between the marine beacons, airways beacons and broadcast stations, it is seldom that a radio direction finder is out of range of at least two or more stations. The advent of very-high-frequency VOR airways omni-ranges, and companion receivers for use on boats, opens an additional means of radio navigation to augment the conventional low-frequency beacons and medium-frequency broadcast stations. Other electronic equipment should include a depth sounder, radiotelephone, automatic pilot, and if the ultimate in safety is desired, radar should be aboard.

TYPES OF BOATS SUITABLE FOR COASTAL CRUISING

There are times when a canoe could be sailed or paddled from the coastal harbors, across their bars and out into the Pacific—

but those times are few and far between, and it is quite unlikely that the Pacific would remain placid enough for the voyager to go from one harbor to the next without running into trouble. Boats little larger than canoes, but designed and built for ocean service and manned by adventurous people, have made long trips up and down the coast, and to the Hawaiian Islands—but again, they are far and few between.

Under favorable weather conditions, and crewed by persons with sea-going experience, well-designed and staunchly built power or sail boats of 30 feet in length can safely be used for coastal cruising. There may be times that they will have to lie at anchor behind a protective headland, or in a harbor, waiting for improved weather conditions; or make a retreat to a sheltered cove if a blow comes up and the going gets rough. There are also times that the heaviest hundred-footer will do the same. Fast, planing-type cruisers have made the trip up the coast, but generally do so in short legs and during early morning hours before normal midday and afternoon winds create a chop or sea condition that forces them to reduce speed.

Power boats should have a minimum cruising range of 150 miles for cruising between San Diego and San Francisco; a minimum of 200 miles when going between San Francisco and Port Orford; and no less than 400 miles' range for the Oregon–Washington sector of the coast.

Passenger ferries are operated by the State of Washington across Puget Sound from Seattle and Everett, and from Anacortes through the San Juan Islands to Sidney on Vancouver Island. They also carry cars and trailers, and are frequently used by those with trailed boats to reach areas in the Hood Canal or the San Juan Islands, where there are scores of launching ramps or lifts; or to reach the Canadian Gulf Islands without traversing the Strait of Juan de Fuca and the Strait of Georgia.

HOUSE-BOATS FOR CHARTER ON DELTA RIVERS

The growing popularity of houseboats has resulted in the establishment of many charter and rental companies in the Delta region. SEA and Pacific Motor Boat magazine carries advertisements by such operators, and is recommended as the best source of information.

APPROXIMATE DISTANCES IN NAUTICAL MILES
BETWEEN PRINCIPAL CALIFORNIA, OREGON &
WASHINGTON POINTS

| | | | Cumulative distances | |
| BETWEEN | | | From San Diego | To Olympia from |
#1	#2	Miles	to col. #2	col. #1
San Diego, Calif.	Oceanside	35	35	1363
Oceanside	Newport	33	68	1328
Newport	Los Angeles	20	88	1295
Los Angeles	Santa Barbara	82	170	1275
Santa Barbara	Coxo Anchorage	35	205	1193
Coxo Anchorage	Port San Luis	51	256	1158
Port San Luis	Morro Bay	21	277	1107
Morro Bay	Monterey	102	379	1086
Monterey	Half Moon Bay	62	441	984
Half-Moon Bay	San Francisco *	24	465	922
San Francisco *	Pt. Reyes	28	493	898
Pt. Reyes	Bodega Bay	23	516	870
Bodega Bay	Shelter Cove	117	633	847
Shelter Cove	Eureka	54	687	730
Eureka	Crescent City	60	747	676
Crescent City	Port Orford, Ore.	65	812	616
Port Orford, Ore.	Coos Bay	51	863	551
Coos Bay	Newport	77	940	500
Newport	Tillamook	55	995	423
Tillamook	Columbia River **	40	1035	368
Columbia River **	Gray's Hbr., Wash.	44	1079	328
Gray's Hbr., Wash.	Cape Flattery	96	1175	284
Cape Flattery	Port Townsend	86	1261	188
Port Townsend	Seattle	40	1301	102
Seattle	Tacoma	25	1326	62
Tacoma	Olympia	37	1363	37

* San Francisco Marina
** Columbia River Lightship
The direct steamer courses between San Diego, Calif., and Olympia, Wash.
cover a distance of 1278 miles, but harbor-hopping, as done in this table
of distances, increases the route to 1363 miles.

PART III

CRUISING BRITISH COLUMBIA AND ALASKA

CHAPTER 1

Broad Aspects

Of all the areas on the Pacific Coast, this region is the most complex and difficult to paint in words. The Inside Passage spans a distance of nearly 1000 miles, between Victoria, B. C. and Juneau, Alaska; it encompasses thousands of islands, fiords that extend into snow-capped canyons with glaciers at their ends, the contrasting capitol cities of British Columbia and Alaska, and salt-water channels so narrow in places that they can only be navigated during a very few minutes of high or low slack water.

Once north of Vancouver, B. C., the economy of the area is almost solely dependent on nature—fishing, lumbering and wood processing or mining. Transportation is only by boat or airplane, with few miles of roads radiating but short distances from such cities or towns as Pender Harbor, Powell River, Prince Rupert, Queen Charlotte, Ketchikan, Wrangell, Petersburg and Juneau. Between these isolated communities are mountain ranges, glaciers, inlets, rivers and bays that make utterly impossible their connection by highways. On Vancouver Island only slightly more than half of the mainland side of the island is linked by good roads, connecting such towns or cities as Victoria, Nanaimo, Port Alberni and Campbell River.

With the exception of Vancouver and Prince Rupert, B. C., every other city, town and fishing village is dependent on water transportation for its major supplies. The machinery and materials to construct buildings and what few miles of roads there are; fuel and lubricants for boats, planes and vehicles; most foods, household furniture and appliances; all are freighted by water from such mainland terminals as Seattle, Vancouver and Prince Rupert. Return cargoes are canned fish, pulp and paper, some finished lumber, and aluminum ingots. In no other region of the North American continent is the economy of the people so dependent on water transportation, augmented by private planes and air carriers.

Entirely new transportation systems have been developed to serve the needs of British Columbia and Alaska. Train-barges towed by Herculean powered tugs carry loaded freight cars and containers as far west as Seward, Alaska where they join the Alaska Railroad system; the Yukon Territory is served by special steamers operating from Vancouver to Skagway, where their cargoes are transferred to the narrow-gauge White Pass and Yukon Railroad; float planes and amphibians carry freight and passengers to areas not served by regularly scheduled surface or air transport.

There are a number of ways to see the wondrous beauty of British Columbia and Alaska. The most pleasurable, of course, is aboard one's own boat. To make the round trip from Victoria, B. C. to Juneau, Alaska, requires time—a minimum of a month, and preferably two months—and even the longer cruise would leave unexplored the vast majority of the region. By the most direct route, the distance is about 950 miles each way; to cruise to the headwaters of only one inlet, such as Princess Louisa, would add 150 miles to the trip, and for each Princess Louisa Inlet, there are scores of others that await exploring.

For those with less time to spare than is needed for cruising their own boats, an alternate means of seeing these waters is from passenger ships which sail on regular schedules from Vancouver, B.C. to as far north as Skagway, roughly 100 miles beyond Juneau. Depending upon the steamship line, stops are made at Prince Rupert, Ketchikan, Wrangell, Petersburg and Juneau. The long summer days, with daylight for an average of seventeen hours, leave only a small part of each twenty-four hours when darkness shuts out the scenery.

A third alternative is to fly aboard modern jetliners from Seattle to Ketchikan and Juneau. From these cities local airlines provide frequent flying-boat service as far west as Sitka on Baranof Island and to intermediate points. In many ways the air trip reveals more of the deep indentations and long inlets than does a trip by boat. Many have made their first trips to Alaska by steamer and returned by air, to get two views of the Inside Passage.

Still another means of cruising parts of British Columbia and Alaska is to use the 1963-instituted car-ferry service of the Alaska Marine Highway System. Three ultra-modern, 350-foot vessels run between Prince Rupert, which is the western terminus of the Canadian Pacific railroad and the Trans-Canada Highway, and

Ketchikan, Wrangell, Petersburg, Juneau, Haines and Skagway. On certain schedules the ferries include Sitka, on the Pacific side of Baranof Island, which was first settled by the Russians in 1799. It was here that the official transfer of Alaska was made from the Russians in 1867.

There are three well-defined cruising areas between Victoria, B. C. and Juneau, Alaska. The first is in the protection of 250-mile-long Vancouver Island, between Victoria-Vancouver and Cape Caution. The Strait of Georgia extends from the southeastern end of the island to approximately its mid-length, with Vancouver on the mainland side of the Strait across from Nanaimo on the island side. The Strait is a large body of water, ranging in width from a few miles to as much as 30 miles. At its north western extremity Quadra and Cortez Islands start an entirely different type of cruising waters that continues northwest to the end of Vancouver Island, across from Cape Caution. To cover this remaining portion of 120 miles, as the seagulls fly, could involve cruising thousands of miles if the many long inlets and bays are visited.

The second major area is between the northwest end of Vancouver Island and Ketchikan, Alaska. To the west are Queen Charlotte Sound and Hecate Strait, with Graham and Moresby Islands from 30 to 60 miles seaward. This portion of a trip can be either the wildest for rough water, going through the Sound and Strait, or the most placid, by taking the back channels in the lee of the islands that fringe the mountainous mainland coastline. No matter how rough it may be outside, the inner Inside Passage is generally lake-smooth.

Cruising from Ketchikan to Juneau, in the third area of the route, is comparable to cruising on the east side of Vancouver Island, in that major islands (such as Prince of Wales, Kupreanof, Admiralty and Baranof) are seaward, giving protection to the winding channels that lie to the east of those islands.

Lest the phrase "winding channels" or "back channels" be misunderstood to mean buoyed and dredged waterways, it should be recognized that the Inside Passage waters of British Columbia and Alaska are deep, extremely so, to within frighteningly close distances to the shores. The biggest problem in navigating these waters is to recognize a point or islet, and to take the correct heading to the next landmark. The options of routes between any two anchorages are so many that cruising these waters is a team operation of helmsman and navigator to avoid becoming almost

Mendenhall Glacier at Juneau, Alaska.

hopelessly lost among the myriad of islands, coves and inlets. True, the principal and shorter routes are well marked with lighted structures on points and shores of islands, each of which is numbered and referenced on the charts—but the many miles of back channels, generally the more picturesque ones, are only well charted.

Fuel and supplies are readily available along the entire Victoria-Juneau route. In British Columbia waters, the Canadian government has built scores of small docks and floats, mainly for their commercial fishermen, but at which pleasure boats can generally tie for the night or even a few days. At some of the most remote island harbors, where there is only a small store for supplies, an oil dock and a few fishermen who maintain homes at the harbor, there will be a post office and communications by radio to Vancouver or Prince Rupert. Much of the shore-based radio communication is by very-high-frequency equipment, which is basically line-of-sight in its range—but there are repeater stations on the mountain tops that result in a network of radio communications that is used by all who need contact with the outside world.

From Petersburg north, even in midsummer, the presence of glaciers at the heads of inlets is evidenced by icebergs in the bays

The floating home and means of livelihood of a fisherman are tied to the banks of landlocked Allison Harbor, British Columbia.

and straits—often many miles away from where they broke off. This need not imply that the weather is cold; to the contrary, summer temperatures range in the 60's, and this warmth is the cause of the break-offs from the glaciers.

Once docked at Juneau, the sportsman can go fishing for 40-pound salmon in Gastineau Channel, on the side of which the capitol city is built; or fly by helicopter to the Alpine-like ski areas atop the Juneau Icecap; or do both within an hour if he chooses. Few other cities of the world can offer this contrast, at a conclusion to a 4000-mile coastal cruise.

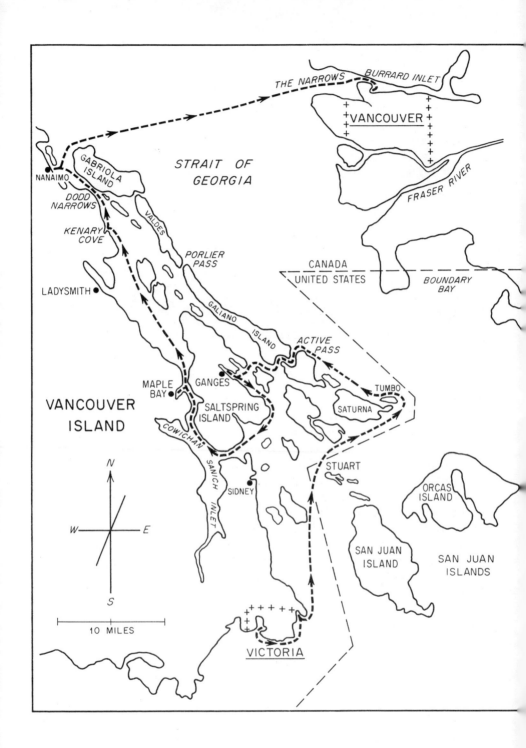

THE NARROWS   BURRARD INLET

+ +
VANCOUVER +
+ +
+ +
+

STRAIT OF
GEORGIA

FRASER RIVER

NANAIMO

GABRIOLA
ISLAND

DODD
NARROWS

VALDES

KENARY
COVE

CANADA
UNITED STATES

BOUNDARY
BAY

LADYSMITH

PORLIER
PASS

GALIANO ISLAND

ACTIVE
PASS

VANCOUVER
ISLAND

MAPLE
BAY

GANGES

SALTSPRING
ISLAND

TUMBO

SATURNA

COWICHAN

STUART

N

ORCAS
ISLAND

W   E

SANICH INLET

SIDNEY

SAN JUAN
ISLAND

SAN JUAN
ISLANDS

S

10 MILES

+ + + + +
+
VICTORIA

CHAPTER 2

Victoria to Vancouver, B. C.

Victoria is the Provincial Capitol of British Columbia, typically British and considerably more so than Vancouver. Situated on the southeastern end of Vancouver Island, it overlooks the Strait of Juan de Fuca to the south, and Haro Strait to the east. Victoria is linked to Port Angeles on the Washington State side of the Strait by ferry, and to Seattle and Vancouver by the venerable Princess steamers.

In the very heart of Victoria, nearly a mile within a completely land-locked waterway, is one of its two fine yacht harbors. The other is at Cadboro Bay, to the northeast of Victoria proper, and enroute to the Gulf Islands that border the Georgia Strait side of Vancouver Island.

The inner harbor has slips and moorings, and all the necessities for cruising are within easy walking distance of the harbor. At the nearby Customs House, the required cruising permits for boats arriving from the States can be quickly obtained. Only a few minutes' walk from the inner harbor is the stately Parliament House, stone-built in true Old English style. On the Causeway, directly across from the harbor, is the impressive Empress Hotel which has hosted Kings and Queens, Presidents and Ambassadors, from all over the world.

Cruising eastward out of Victoria's snug harbor puts one immediately into the waters on which Capt. Vancouver sailed in the era of his discovery and survey of Puget Sound and the Strait of Georgia, some 170 years ago. Hugging the island coastline, we pass close by Trial Island light, and turn north into Cadboro Bay where the Royal Victoria Yacht Club has its facilities. Slips and anchorages are available to visiting yachts, and fuel and supplies are obtainable if they were not taken aboard in Victoria's inner harbor.

To the east of Cadboro Bay, across Haro Strait, it is less than

191

Victoria, British Columbia, Haro Strait and the San Juan Archipelago. Far background is continuously snow-capped Mount Baker.

10 miles to San Juan Island, the westernmost of the San Juan Archipelago. Our cruise takes us into Haro Strait, but to the northwest around Cadboro Point toward the first of the Gulf Islands, frequently called Canadian San Juan Islands (which are virtually a continuation of those in the stateside waters). We will remain in Canadian waters until past Prince Rupert, nearly 450 miles toward Alaska.

The choice of routes through the Gulf Islands, toward Nanaimo, is as varied as the hundreds of islands that make up the group. They cover an area that is 20 miles in width at the widest point, and roughly 50 miles long in a northwesterly direction. The larger ones and many of the smaller ones are like a mountain range, with their ridges extending up from the clear waters of the Strait of Georgia; and between their ends are narrow pas-

Cadboro Bay, Victoria, B. C.

sages from the inner channels to the broad Strait. Many of the smaller ones are privately owned, and on one trip in this area we were invited to spend the weekend with the then owners of Tumbo Island. This lies to the east of Saturna Island, with a narrow channel between it and Saturna, and on the opposite side the wide expanse of the Strait.

Our instructions were very explicit, "approach Tumbo Island from the east, keeping Rosenfelt Rock buoy to your port side; when abeam the islet with the tall firs, stop a few hundred yards off shore and we will send a pilot out in a small boat to guide you into the inner harbor."

We had left Cadboro Bay earlier in the afternoon, cruised northerly past Stuart Island of the San Juan group, South Pender Island of the Canadian group, and the east end of Saturna Island.

Total distance to this point was roughly 35 miles, and the Rosen-felt Rock buoy was in sight. Rounding it from the eastward, we proceeded as directed for another 2 miles, and soon saw a launch (as they are called in Canada) coming out from the islet. When hailed by the young lad who was running the launch, we stopped and welcomed aboard an elderly gentleman whom he had brought to act as our pilot. His first statement when stepping on deck was "please take me to the pilot house"—which seemed odd, and when there he told us to take a heading of 340 degrees "until you see the white rock on the far side of the inner channel"; when it came into sight he said, "When you see the white rock, turn left to 250 degrees until the patch of kelp is close by your starboard side." Just when we were coming to the kelp, and within a hundred feet of a group of rocks on our port said, he said, "When you pass the kelp, make a slow, easy turn, to head you toward the barn on the bank of the channel." By now all of us were becoming curious as to why he should be wearing dark glasses in the late afternoon, but were too concerned about his instructions to ask any questions. When nearly within touching distance of the channel bank, his next order was "Head her to-ward the floats at the head of the bay, and drop your anchor when opposite the tallest tree on the point just off your port bow." This we did, and anchored in 2 fathoms of water, with towering trees on all but the open channel side. It was not till then that he introduced himself, and apologized for his gruffness, but added "You certainly do a fine job of obeying orders from the only blind pilot in Canadian waters!" Were we relieved to be at anchor!

Two days with our friends, the owners of the island, were filled with clam digging and oyster picking, intermingled with some salmon fishing in Tumbo Channel. We wanted to prolong our stay at Tumbo, but friends were to meet us at Maple Bay on Vancouver Island for the trip to Nanaimo and Vancouver. This led us to Active Pass, 10 miles from Tumbo Island on the north-western end of Mayne Island, as a means of getting from the Strait of Georgia to the westward of Saltspring Island, largest of the Gulf Island group. Active Pass is well named because it car-ries both a tremendous volume of water in and out of the Strait of Georgia with each change of tide, and much of the pleasure and commercial traffic between Vancouver and Victoria. It is an S-shaped channel, well marked, relatively narrow but breathtakingly beautiful, with tree-covered hills and peaks as high as a thousand feet within a mile of the passage.

Enroute from Active Pass to Maple Bay (and only three miles off our most direct route) is the very complete harbor of Ganges on Saltspring Island. There we took on fuel and water, replenished the larder with fresh vegetables and fine meats, and could have played golf on their attractive course if time had permitted. Retracing our course out of Ganges Harbor, we kept Saltspring Island on our starboard hand, passing Fulford Harbor on the Island; passed Sanich Inlet, which cuts deeply into Vancouver Island and with its southern end almost reaching the outskirts of Victoria; and finally turned northwest, past Cowichan Bay, to the narrow channel that leads to Maple Bay. A small bight off the north side of Cowichan Bay, named Genoa Bay, is the site of the Cowichan Bay Yacht Club with floats and fine shore-side facilities. Genoa Bay is also well known for summer resort attractions that include an outdoor, heated swimming pool, lodges, a pitch-and-putt golf course, tennis courts, restaurants, and rental boats for local fishing, all in addition to fuel and ship stores.

Many have cruised past Maple Bay without realizing it exists, because it is tucked into a small inlet off the main route toward Nanaimo. We had it well circled on our *Northwest Cruising Atlas* and had a specific date with friends to meet them at the Maple Bay Yacht Club. Although there are floats for visiting boats, a more startling view of the evergreen-timbered mountains rising from the water's edge can be had when anchored in the bay. We had been towing our dinghy, which presents no problem in these protected waters, and in a few strokes of the oars were ashore. Later we rowed the less than 200 yards to the south end of the bay, lest we disturb the quiet of the evening with even the small noise of the outboard engine. There, in the crystal-clear waters, all manner of fish were leisurely swimming under the dinghy, almost challenging us to tempt them with a trolling line.

Twenty miles northwest of Maple Bay, past countless islands to our right and the coal-mining town of Ladysmith on Vancouver Island to our left, we had another date with friends. It was at Boat Harbor, also known as Kenary Cove, where visitors are sometimes greeted with the firing of cannons. On other occasions, when friends of the one-family community are arriving, the host will serenade them with music from his high fidelity outdoor loudspeakers that can be heard throughout the entire half-mile-wide cove. He may also invite them to see his growing collection of antique firearms, and Indian artifacts that he has found in the nearby caves.

Many years ago the harbor was used for log rafting by lumber operators who would tow their rafts to mills in Nanaimo or Ladysmith. Now, the only reminders of its commercial days are the remains of a pier and a few pilings that were used to corral the logs dumped into the cove.

Across from Kenary Cove is a chain of small islands, and beyond them are big Valdez and Gabriola Islands, which separate this cruising region from the Strait of Georgia. Between Valdez and Gabriola Islands is one of the three main passes between the Strait and the area we have been cruising, named Gabriola Pass. Like Porlier and Active Passes, to the southeast, Gabriola is a winding one through which currents of up to 8 knots will flow during the ebb and flood tides.

Taking leave from our host at Kenary Cove, we proceed to Dodd Narrows, timing our arrival at slack water. This is one of the narrowest in this island group, and unless one wants a thrill of shooting the rapids, or trying to buck them, it is prudent to use the tide tables to establish the time of passing Joan Point in Dodd Narrows. The biggest danger of going through the Narrows other than at reasonably slack water is the risk of tangling with driftwood or floating logs, which gyrate with the current and eddies and are completely unpredictable as to direction, combined with the problem of maneuvering one's own boat in the currents to avoid logs.

From the Narrows to Nanaimo is only 6 miles. This fine harbor is frequently the first official stop for those cruising from the States to British Columbia, for cruising permits can be obtained here at the Customs House. The officers make a brief inspection of the boat, checking on firearms and any oversupply of "spirits." Substantial floating docks that can accommodate as many as a dozen visiting boats at one time are directly below the main street of Nanaimo, and it is only a few minutes walk to any type of desired store—for foods, Canadian "spirits," ship's supplies or other cruising necessities.

Overlooking the harbor is the old Block House, once heavily fortified to defend Nanaimo from Indians and pirates. It is both a landmark and a museum. Shipyards, oil docks and additional visitor-boat floats are a mile to the northwest of the city-center floats, on the west side of Newcastle Island Passage. The Nanaimo

Nanaimo, Port of Entry into British Columbia, on Vancouver Island.

Yacht Club also has its splendid facilities in this Passage, which leads to Departure Bay where there is ample room for those wishing to anchor instead of tying to floating docks.

Thirty-three miles to the northeast, across the Strait of Georgia, is the largest of British Columbia's cities—Vancouver, named after the Captain whose sailing ship *Discovery* first entered the harbor in 1792. The main links between Nanaimo and Vancouver are high-speed ferry boats, coastal-type freighters and towed barges. To the south of Vancouver the 500-mile-long Fraser River empties into the Strait through three mouths, the largest and most used being about 10 miles from the Burrard Inlet entrance to Vancouver. During the spring and summer run-off the silt carried down the river is evident in the Strait for many miles from its mouths.

For power boats, the trip across the Strait is best made in the mornings, because afternoon winds from either the northwest or southeast through the Strait can create a miserable beam-sea condition. For sailing, the afternoons are better.

After passing under Lions Gate Bridge, at the first narrows, the inner harbor of Vancouver rudely awakens one from his cruising thoughts. It teems with traffic—luxury liners on world cruises, outboard-powered fishing skiffs, freighters destined for far-off ports, power and sailing yachts, tugs pulling mile-long log rafts to the mills in the upper reaches of the harbor. For the benefit of large vessels entering or departing, in the center of the bridge span are traffic signal lights—to tell the pilots what other traffic may be approaching the bridge from the opposite direction!

Burrard Inlet, spanned by Lions Gate Bridge, extends more than twenty miles past Vancouver. It creates current conditions that can pose steering problems for long tows or large vessels.

Once inside the narrows, it is only 3 miles to the extensive docks and floats of the Royal Vancouver and Burrard Yacht Clubs, both situated on the edge of Stanley Park.

Deeply forested Stanley Park, center, adjoins the Yacht Harbour at Vancouver, B. C.

Unique to Vancouver harbor are the fueling barges, anchored in the bay about 1 mile from the two yacht clubs, which handle a large proportion of the fueling for Vancouver's large pleasure boat fleet as well as much of the smaller-size commercial craft. The barges are roughly 60 to 80 feet square, with enormous rubber-tire fenders around the four sides to protect the boats taking on fuel from the considerable amount of motion created by the nearly continuous water traffic passing them. In addition to fuel, they also dispense bottled gas for galley ranges, and fresh water. When the oil barges (as they are called) are busy, with boats tied to all four sides of each barge, the traffic jams created by the boats waiting to tie alongside can test the skill of the most competent skipper!

After fueling we proceeded to the Burrard Yacht Club, where we were greeted with the deep-throated whistle of a steam tug that had been converted to pleasure cruising. The clanging of its engine-room bells, as it maneuvered to make room for us, was reminiscent of an era when steam was supreme, and all aboard our cruiser expressed admiration for the owner of the steamer for his interest in keeping alive the type of vessel which had played such an important part in building the northwest.

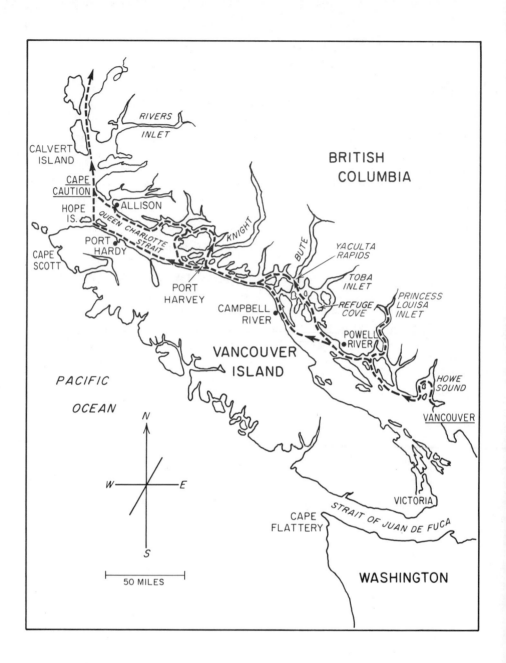

RIVERS
INLET

CALVERT
ISLAND

BRITISH
COLUMBIA

CAPE
CAUTION

HOPE
IS.

ALLISON

QUEEN CHARLOTTE STRAIT

KNIGHT

BUTE

YACULTA
RAPIDS

CAPE
SCOTT

PORT
HARDY

TOBA
INLET

PORT
HARVEY

CAMPBELL
RIVER

REFUGE
COVE

PRINCESS
LOUISA
INLET

VANCOUVER
ISLAND

POWELL
RIVER

PACIFIC

OCEAN

N

HOWE
SOUND

VANCOUVER

W   E

VICTORIA

S

CAPE
FLATTERY

STRAIT OF JUAN DE FUCA

50 MILES

WASHINGTON

CHAPTER 3

Vancouver, B. C. to Cape Caution

The cruising waters in the lee of Vancouver Island, between Vancouver and Cape Caution, are ones to enjoy on a leisurely basis. The direct route is about 250 miles, but on the indirect routes one could cover 10,000 miles and never anchor twice in the same bight, cove or inlet. Traveling at only 10 knots, the round trip could be made in four days—but forty days could be spent in exploring these protected waters and only part of them would be visited.

It is within the lee of Vancouver Island that there are such well-known inlets as Jervis, Princess Louisa, Toba, Bute, Knight, Belize and Seymour—just to name a few—all on the mainland side to the northeast of the Island.

Our most recent cruise through these waters was with a group of other power boats from Seattle and Vancouver, with a destination of Juneau. The daily runs were from 40 to 90 miles, and at the end of each day everyone had the same feeling: "If only we could have taken time to go up this inlet or that inlet—or to have laid over for a week in just one of the many groups of islands."

Heading westward from Vancouver's Lions Gate bridge, there is a contrast of views that should be noted. Looking astern, past the bridge, are city skyscrapers; to the north are snow-capped mountains that literally jump out of the Strait of Georgia; to the west is the entrance to Howe Sound; and to the south the 30-mile span of Georgia Strait.

Howe Sound has become one of Vancouver yachtsmen's favor- ite cruising and resort areas. It is only 6 miles from the bridge to the eastern side of the entrance to the Sound. Extending 22 miles into mountains, the Sound is filled with four large islands and a dozen smaller ones, all heavily timbered and indented with some 30 anchorages. Many of the anchorages or coves have visitor floats,

Looking north toward Gambier Island in Howe Sound, a popular cruising area for Vancouver, B. C.'s yachtsmen because of its close proximity and well protected, island-studded waters.

and there are more than a half-dozen fueling stations for local and visiting craft. During summer months, many Vancouver businessmen commute to their summer homes on the Sound, tying their boats to floats or mooring them to buoys.

Thirty-five miles northwest of Howe Sound, with Half Moon Bay and Thormanby Islands enroute, is Pender Harbor, which might easily be passed without noticing the 3-mile deep indentation into the surrounding hills, from the Strait of Georgia. A mile inside the Harbor, on the north side, is a cove that provides excellent anchorage, close to floats that lead to the lodge on the shore. On one side of this cove is a marine railway and boat repair facility, with a high-roofed shed over the ways for protection from their heavy winter rains. The village of Pender Harbor is on the north side of the channel just after entering the bight. This is frequently the point where those cruising through Jervis Inlet will take on their extra fuel and other ship's needs, because it is easy to cruise 150 miles between Pender Harbor and Westview, near Powell River, without passing another major supply depot.

One of the most photographed waterfalls in British Columbia

is Chatterbox Falls, at the extreme upper reaches of Princess Louisa Inlet. Reaching it from Pender Harbor takes us through the Agamemnon Channel with Seechelt Peninsula close by our starboard. On the eastern side of the Peninsula is Seechelt Inlet with its Skookumchuck Narrows four miles from the Inlet's convergence with Agamemnon Channel. Passage through the Narrows should only be made at or near slack water because a body of water 40 miles in length must pass through the ⅛-mile-wide Narrows with each change of tide. Velocities reach as high as 12 knots. A convenient place to wait for slack water is at Egmont, where fuel and supplies are available and substantial floating docks are maintained.

One of the few sand beaches in this areas is a mile northeast of Egmont Point, on Wales Reach, an extension of Jervis Inlet. Anchorage can be taken close to shore, off the sand beach. Another good anchoring spot is behind Sydney Island, across Wales Reach from Egmont Point. From here, up through Wales, Princess Royal and Queen's Reaches, the water is deep and most boats will tie alongside log booms, instead of trying to anchor.

Princess Louisa Inlet is 6 miles from the northwestern limits of Queens Reach, and extends 4 miles northeasterly between 5- to 8-thousand-foot mountains. Entrance to it should be timed with slack water, to avoid the thrills of going with or bucking 8- to 10-knot currents through its narrow, S-shaped channel, at the mouth of the Inlet. Inside and to port is Malibu Lodge, with guest accommodations, restaurant, some provisions for boats and a fuel dock. This Inlet, too, is extremely deep—in many places over 1000 feet deep—but at its end are floats for visiting boats, virtually the only spot in the Inlet where anchoring is practical. The roaring Chatterbox Falls have created a small sandbar that extends a few hundred yards from the water's edge, with depths shallow enough for anchoring. The current created by the Falls holds an anchored boat with its bow toward shore.

For nearly thirty years, much of Princess Louisa Inlet was owned by James F. Macdonald, an ardent boatsman and lover of wilderness beauty. During the summers he lived aboard his houseboat, tied to the floats he had built, and was the genial host to yachtsmen from every port of the Pacific Coast. In 1953 he deeded the property to The Princess Louisa International Society, which was formed by a group of Canadian and American yachtsmen to preserve the area in its natural state. The Society

Chatterbox Falls rushes down from its perpetual ice-cap source to dilute the salt water of Princess Louisa Inlet just the right amount for oyster propagation.

deeded it back to the Canadian government in 1964 with the stipulation it could never be commercialized, and must always be kept "in natural" as a marine park.

Returning downstream to the Strait of Georgia, we head north-east toward Powell River, across from the northerly end of 30-mile-long Texada Island. The largest pulp and paper mills in British Columbia are located here, and much of their output is shipped to publishers in the United States as newsprint paper. The actual port of entry for Powell River is Westview, two miles to the southeast, where there is a government-built small-boat harbor with fuel, supplies, marine railway and repair facilities. It is a short ride by taxi to Powell River and visitors are invited to go on the conducted tours through the pulp and paper mills.

From Powell River or Westview to Cape Caution there is the choice of the inside-Inside Passage route through the Yaculta Rapids or the shorter route through Seymour Narrows. If the Seymour Narrows route is chosen, a straight run of about 30 miles is made across the Strait of Georgia to Cape Mudge on Quadra Island; if the inside route is chosen, it will be close by the mainland shoreline to the eastern side of Cortes Island and

Floats are provided for pleasure craft at Princess Louisa's terminus of Chatterbox Falls.

Looking south to Strait of Georgia, across Buccaneer Bay on Thormanby Island.

through Lewis Channel. Our last trip was through the inside route and even though considerably longer in distance, it provided greater opportunities to visit back-channel communities and anchorages.

An easy run of about 22 miles takes us from Westview to Refuge Cove on Redondo Island. The first to arrive ties alongside floats, and those arriving later merely put over fenders and raft to the first, second, third or fourth boat out from the floats. Typical of so many of these British Columbia anchorages, there will be floats for a half-dozen or more boats, gasoline and diesel fuel, and a small supply store either on a barge or built on pilings at the water's edge. Not infrequently, high-octane aviation fuel is also available for the many float planes that are flown in this area. Generally there will be a few commercial trollers also in the anchorage and almost without exception the opportunity to buy for pennies a freshly caught salmon. A small islet in the entrance to Refuge Cove gives it added protection from winds, and assures a mirror-like water condition in the Cove. Five miles to the east is Deep Bay, where at low tide some of the finest clams are to be had; and to the northeast is Toba Inlet that stretches over twenty miles into the mountains.

Some 18 miles northwest of Refuge Cove is Stuart Island, where another choice must be made—whether to enter 35-mile-deep Bute Inlet on the east side of the Island, or stay on schedule to meet the slack water in Yaculta Rapids. The latter requires considerable figuring, because there is a series of rapids in the 5 miles between Stuart Island and the Dent Islands to the west; there is also a difference of about a half-hour in the times of slack waters at the two ends of the rapids. When correctly calculated, the passage can be as smooth as glass, albeit with considerable traffic during the cruising season, because pleasure, fishing and commercial boats all wait for the slack water to go through Yaculta Rapids.

Westward of the Rapids a myriad of channels can be taken to Port Harvey, roughly 60 miles distant. Ever since the 1964 earthquake which did so much damage to western Alaska (nearly 1000 miles from the area we are now cruising), the times of maximum currents have been considerably changed from what they were before the earthquake. The times of maximum flood velocities have not been changed as much as maximum ebb, which occurs now as much as $1\frac{1}{2}$ hours later than formerly. For those on predicted-log contests through this route, this has thrown another variable into their predictions.

Leaving the inner-Inside Passage through Sunderland Channel puts us on a 15-mile stretch of Johnstone Strait, which is also part of the Vancouver to Cape Caution route through Seymour Narrows. A turn to the north, however, leads us into Port Harvey and again on the waters of the inside-Inside Passage. Within Port Harvey is a near-deserted lumbering operation, with a group of government-provided floats for tying alongside. From this cove to Minstrel Island, where fuel and ship stores are available, a winding course through Chatham Channel must be made. It is one of the few channels in this region where the shoreline does not rise abruptly from the water; instead, there are marshy flats for ¼ mile or more on the easterly side of the channel. Also unusual is the kelp, which grows in the shallower waters despite the currents that range as high as 7 knots.

Minstrel Island is a jumping-off point for cruising Knight Inlet, which reaches 50 miles northeasterly into snow-capped mountains. In the opposite direction, Knight Inlet extends 30 miles before reaching Queen Charlotte Strait. Twelve miles from

Typical of the thousands of islets dotting Inside Passage waters is this one near Allison Harbor, British Columbia.

Minstrel, on the northern banks of Knight Inlet is Hoeya Sound, which is reported to have exceptionally fine crabs. From there to its headwaters there are few clearly defined anchorages, due to the depths in the Inlet; hence, it is not an infrequent sight to see a boat with bow and stern lines tied to trees on the banks of a slight indentation. Literally hundreds of waterfalls cascade down the steep ravines, and the amount of fresh water pouring into the Inlet maintains a slight down-channel current at all times.

To travel the 55-mile distance, as the seagulls fly, between Minstrel and Allison Harbor, takes us through some 50 miles of winding, island-studded channels to Queen Charlotte Sound—and 25 miles of open-water cruising. Since leaving Vancouver, this is the longest stretch of open water we have covered, yet it is reasonably protected by the northwestern end of Vancouver Island, 15 miles to the westward. It can be, however, a rough stretch of water if a strong northwest wind is blowing down the Sound.

Allison Harbor is no more than a small, wooded cove, with floats for visiting boats, fuel, and a general store on a barge tied to the banks of the cove. A path leads into the forest for those

Single-filing through Schooner Passage to its headwaters of Nakwakto Rapids, where currents race up to 24 knots at full ebb or rise.

who like hiking, and wild berries of many kinds can be picked within a few yards of the shoreline. Our fleet filled the harbor, and before long wisps of smoke from galley ranges or barbecues filled the evening air with the aroma of cooking steaks and salmon. An early morning departure was agreed upon by the skippers to make the run through Schooner Passage to Nakwakto Rapids.

Although we started in sunshine, our vista ahead was soon shrouded in fog. Radar-equipped boats led our single-file procession as we slid and slewed against a 5-knot current through the winding Passage. Moving in and out of fog veils, it was an eerie sight, reminiscent of one of Hitchock's dramatic "fog-on-the-moors" effects. A half-hour's time, during which the smaller boats, even at full throttle, were often pushed sidewise by eddies and currents, brought our fleet to a pool of still water. Here, Schooner Passage and Slingsby Channel meet the entrance to Seymour and Belize Inlets. It is at the entrance to the Inlets that the awesome Nakwakto Rapids are situated. They are said to be the fastest and most dangerous in British Columbia. Velocities as high as 24 knots are reached during maximum ebb or flood, to fill or empty the bodies of water that extend eastward from the Rapids for nearly 40 miles. At the time we reached this point the ebb was near the end of its cycle, and water was rushing through the $1/4$-mile narrows at 12 to 14 knots. The braver skippers, with fast cruisers, turned from the quiet pool where the fleet was gathered and with full throttles pushed their way into the Rapids to find a change of more than 6 feet in water level in the $1/2$-mile-long passage through the fast water.

Turning westward from the Rapids, our route was through 5-mile-long Slingsby Channel to the open waters of Queen Charlotte Sound, 8 miles from Cape Caution. This ended the inside-Inside Passage from Vancouver to the Cape, the alternate to the more direct route from Powell River to the Cape, through Seymour Narrows.

As mentioned earlier, the distance from Powell River across the Strait of Georgia to Cape Mudge on Quadra Island is about 30 miles. From there northwestward is again the Inside Passage, in many places as narrow as the back-channel route. It is the route taken by commercial traffic and pleasure craft bent on reaching Alaska in the shortest time. The famous salmon-fishing waters of the Campbell River region are to port, as we pass April

Point and its hidden harbor. Six miles past Campbell River are Seymour Narrows, which until a few years ago were a threat to navigation because of Ripple Rocks in the narrowest part of the Narrows. The Canadian government tunneled under the Narrows and detonated the largest non-atomic explosive charge in history, to remove the Rocks. Although the currents through the Narrows still reach 4 to 6 knots at maximum flow, there are not the violent eddies, whirlpools and crosscurrents that there were before removal of Ripple Rocks.

Once above Seymour Narrows, Discovery Passage and Johnstone Strait average from a mile to three miles in width, with few harbors on the Vancouver Island side of the channels. To the northeast, however, there are scores of inlets, arms and bays that provide good anchorage or the opportunity to tie to government floats. At the entrance to Queen Charlotte Strait is Malcolm Island, with the well-protected Mitchell and Rough Bays on its south side. On the latter is the Finnish community of Sointula, nestled behind a breakwater that protects its small-boat facilities. It is a haven for many cruising north or south because of the hospitality of its residents, sauna baths and fine Finnish foods at its restaurants.

Four miles before reaching Malcolm Island is Alert Bay on Cormorant Island. It is the largest community along this portion of the Inside Passage, with more than a thousand residents— about half of whom are Indian. A number of shipyards and machine shops are available for repair of transient boats or those that make this their home port.

Once past Cormorant and Malcolm Islands, it is 16 miles to Hardy Bay on the Vancouver Island side of the Strait, where supplies of most types are available. The direct route from Port Hardy to Cape Caution, roughly 35 miles, is mainly open water through Queen Charlotte Strait and Queen Charlotte Sound, with Nigei and Hope Islands close by the Vancouver Island shore to the west. Both Islands have numerous small anchorages, and at a number of them, fuel and supplies can be obtained. Village Bay on Hope Island is best known for its cemetery-in-the-trees. High in the trees surrounding the small harbor are cedar-chest coffins, with shakes over them for protection, lashed to the boughs of the trees with rope made from bark. This was a custom of the Indians many years ago, and is unique to this area.

Cape Caution was well named, for it is halfway between the

protection of Calvert Island to the northwest, and the harbors within Queen Charlotte Strait to the southeast. To the west of the Cape is wide-open Queen Charlotte Sound and the entire Pacific Ocean beyond. Cruising either north or south, most skippers chose to round Cape Caution as early in the day as possible, to avoid the normal afternoon build-up of seas that can be expected even during the best of summer weather.

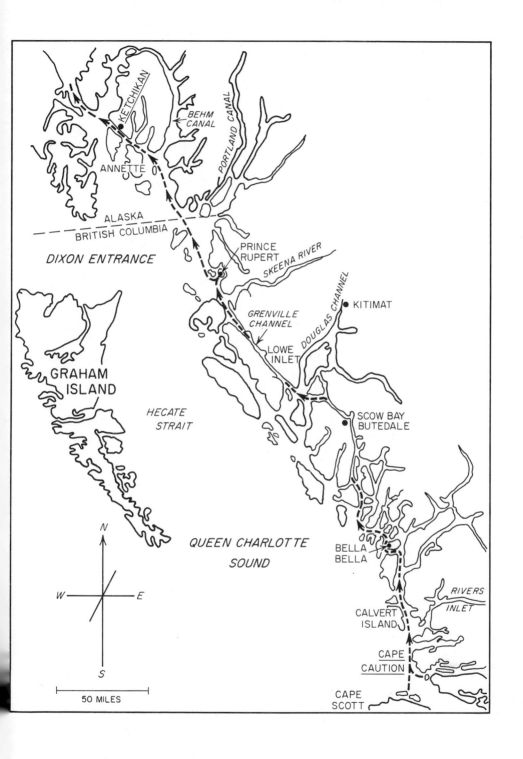

CHAPTER 4

Cape Caution, B. C. to Ketchikan, Alaska

Using Cape Caution, across from the northwest tip of Vancouver Island, as a take-off point for the cruise to Ketchikan, has been done more as a matter of geographical convenience than from a practical cruising standpoint. It is the natural end to the inside-Inside Passages that lie to the east of Vancouver Island, and in a way is the beginning of a somewhat different type of boating, through more open waters and straighter channels.

Popular overnight anchorages before passing Cape Caution are on the mainland side at Allison Harbor, or any one of the dozen or more others in that immediate area, or from the harbors on either Hope or Nigei Islands, snuggled next to Vancouver Island. Cascade Harbor on Nigei Island provides a straight run to the Cape, and from anchor there, Queen Charlotte Sound can be seen. If it looks rough, delay departure—if smooth, get underway as soon as possible! It is about the same distance to Cape Caution from Allison Harbor, although the open-water run is a few miles shorter.

From either Allison or Cascade Harbors, there is a 40-mile stretch of Queen Charlotte Sound that must be covered before reaching the lee of Calvert Island, and the protected waters that are beyond it in Fitzhugh Sound. However, even before reaching Calvert Island there are a number of inlets to the east that are both good refuge as well as magnificent cruising. Time permitting, 55-mile-long Rivers Inlet, with its entrance about 14 miles past Cape Caution, should be cruised. It is filled with little bights, coves and subinlets. At Wadhams, just after entering Rivers Inlet, there is a cannery with fuel and supplies, and on some occasions, an opportunity to can the salmon caught while cruising in this area.

Moving up Fitzhugh Sound in the protection of Calvert and Hunter Islands to port, the biggest navigational hazards are the

214

gillnetters, with their 1000-foot-long gill nets streamed across the channels. Within a distance of possibly 20 miles, we passed scores of these small commercial fishermen, and had to be on constant alert to avoid nets that are marked only with small floats. Tucked into coves, such as at Namu, are canneries operated only a few weeks out of the twelve months, during the salmon-fishing season. Highly mechanized, they are the lifeblood of the economy in this area. During the government-controlled, short fishing season, a stream of cannery tenders from Prince Rupert and Vancouver supply the canneries with empty cans, supplies, fuel, personnel —and bring back to the home ports cases of canned salmon for reshipment to the markets of the world.

From Cape Calvert to within a few miles of Bella Bella, the cruising is through well-protected waters with only a minimum of chart work necessary—we merely steer through the middle of deep channels, with mountains rising from the water on each side.

Bella Bella, on the east side of its channel, and New Bella Bella (which is mainly Indian populated) across the channel are both typical fishing communities. Government floats that will accommodate twenty or thirty boats at one time, a fuel dock, a fish-buying station on a barge are the scene of tremendous activity for a few months of the year—then lie quietly for the balance of the year. At the head of a steeply inclined ramp is the general

Our fleet, tied to the Government floats at Bella Bella, British Columbia.

store where everything (nearly literally) from frozen foods to wearing apparel is available. Even a radio station, for communication from this isolated community to mainland metropolises, is among its modern facilities.

We had occasion to use this radio to order a new air compressor from Seattle, to replace one that failed and left us without windshield wipers or horns. Until it reached us at Juneau, we improvised a system of lines and pulleys around the flying-bridge structure to the three windshield wipers on the forward windows. When we had to use the wipers, two of our crew would alternately pull on the port and starboard lines to give the helmsman the clear visibility he needed.

An easy run of 38 miles, of which about half was nearly straight courses, took us from Bella Bella, through Milbanke Sound to Klemtu on Swindle Island. The last 5 miles was through a channel sometimes only 1/4-mile wide, with timbered mountains rising so fast from the water's edge that it was a continuous wonder how the trees could hang on to the precipitous terrain. We called this "canyon cruising," and continued past Klemtu for another 40 miles to Butedale.

Rounding a point just before reaching Butedale brought into view a cascade of water tumbling down a cut in the hills behind Butedale. The falls come from a lake about 1 mile back from the cove, and possibly 500 feet higher. Besides providing a spectacular sight, the lake is also the source of hydro-electric power at this cannery village.

This was a busy cove during our brief stay, with three amphibian flights arriving and leaving with passengers and mail, fishing boats unloading their catches at the cannery, and a continuous stream of boats in and away from the fueling docks. During the fishing season, the floats are unofficially reserved for the commercial fishermen, who count every minute that they are away from their fishing grounds as lost money—their stops at Butedale are the briefest possible to unload fish, reload fuel and supplies, and be underway again. Our schedule was like theirs; while the wives obtained additional galley supplies, the men fueled and watered their boats in the fastest possible time to make room for the next boat wanting float space.

Only 5 miles away was Scow Bay on Klekane Inlet. That was our destination for the night, where our fleet tied to the remains of a log-rafting boom that had seen many years of profitable service when logging operations were the principal activities of this cove. Now, only the cries of birds or the splashing of jumping fish break the silence.

A small stream empties into Scow Bay, and the crystal-clear water showed crabs practically covering the sand bottom below our rafted cruisers. It was not long before traps were over the sides, and within minutes they were filled; only the largest were kept, and females returned to the cold, clear waters. For some strange reason, within an hour the crabs moved away—and those first caught were the last.

Leaving Scow Bay, we continued the canyon cruising toward Grenville Channel, which is over 40 miles long and only in a few places more than 1 mile wide. At the entrance to Grenville Channel, branching off to starboard is Douglas Channel. Forty-five miles up this winding body of water is the largest industrial community along all of the British Columbia coast, north of Vancouver. It is Kitimat, which has grown from nothing to more than 10,000 population since 1951 when the first buildings were erected. The Aluminium Company of Canada has one of the world's largest aluminum plants at Kitimat, and it is said that upwards of 25,000 persons will be living and working here within the near future. It is a "company town," with piers for ocean-going freighters, floats for small craft, and shipyard and repair facilities for those in need of them.

It is not an unusual sight in Grenville Channel, or the many other channels like it, to see two and sometimes three fishing boats lashed together and proceeding full-speed with only one man at one of the wheels. Engines on the other boats will be working full-bore, but the crews will be sleeping or catching up on rest while traveling between fishing areas.

There are five inlets on the mainland side of Grenville Channel, each with its own brand of secluded charm. Lowe Inlet is one of the most often visited because of the waterfall that pours from the lake at the head of the Inlet, and which draws to it salmon of enormous size. Aside from one fisherman's cabin in the cove, there is no evidence that man has ever found this sanctuary of calm, tree-encircled water.

Roughly 30 miles northwestward of the end of Grenville Channel is Prince Rupert. Approaching it from the south takes us across a 10-mile open stretch of the lower portion of Chatham Sound. To the west are the open waters of Dixon Entrance. This area can be rough, but if too much so, there are scores of anchorages after leaving Grenville Channel and before reaching the Sound.

The change from uncrowded cruising waters to the activity at Prince Rupert forces one to realize that there must be commerce and business to make possible the enjoyment of cruising. Passenger steamers, ocean-going freighters, cannery tenders, fishing boats of all types, mingled with pleasure craft, stream in and out of the harbor. This is the fishing industry's center for the upper British Columbia waters, and is well provided with natural protection from nearby islands. Marine railways, a grid for boats up to 110 feet in length, and supply stores of all types are near the small-craft basins. (On Wednesdays the city's business establishments are closed, so cruising itineraries should contemplate this custom.)

The city is on an island only 4 miles by 6 miles in extent, with seven peaks on it between 1000 and 2300 feet high. Railroad and automobile bridges connect Prince Rupert with the mainland to the east. Across the harbor is the modern airport, on Digby Island.

Before boats leave Prince Rupert, the Canadian cruising permits obtained at Victoria or Vancouver when entering Canadian waters from the States must be turned in to the Customs officials. (When returning from Alaska, cruising toward the States, it is here that the Canadian cruising permits are obtained which are then surrendered at the last port of call in British Columbia before clearing into a State of Washington port of entry.)

A narrow, winding, but well-marked channel around the north end of Digby Island can be used when leaving Prince Rupert. It is well to follow local fishing boats through this channel until past the Indian village of Metlakatla, because of their knowledge of the best parts of the channel to use. For larger boats, the better route away from Prince Rupert is south through the main entrance channel until clear of the many islets off the south end of Digby Island, then into the open waters of Chatham Sound. This is the route used by the Alaska Highway System's passenger car ferries, which link the trans-Canada highway with Alaska's highways at Haines.

The first half of the 85-mile route to Ketchikan is through open water, although there are islands to the westward which give fair protection to the otherwise straight running. But like most of the other sounds and wider straits, there are anchorages in coves along the islands or on the eastern shores, never more than

5 miles distant. Thirty-five miles north of Prince Rupert is the International boundary between Canada and the United States, much of which is shown on charts as running midchannel up Pearse Canal and Portland Inlet to its headwaters, then from mountain peak to mountain peak.

Until within 25 miles of Ketchikan the courses are straight for distances of 10 to 20 miles at a time, until the south tip of Revillagigedo Island is reached. It is on the southwest side of this Island that Ketchikan is situated, on Tongass Narrows. The other three sides of the 45-mile-long Island are surrounded by the Behm Canal, with hundreds of miles of shoreline created by the many deep inlets running into either the Island or the mainland. Near the northern turning point of the Canal is Bell Island Hot Springs, with mineral baths, resort accommodations and limited supplies.

To the west of the south entrance to Behm Canal is Annette Island. On it are two extremes that are typical of Alaska: a modern jet-age airport for trunk-line passengers arriving in or leaving Ketchikan, and the nearly 100-year-old Indian fishing community of Metlakatla with its well-protected harbor behind a recently built breakwater. Within a 2-mile walking distance of Metlakatla are a dozen lakes, ranging in elevation from a few hundred feet

Entering Ketchikan Harbor.

to over 1000 feet, that are favorite fresh-water fishing spots for both residents and visitors to this region.

Across Clarence Strait to the west of Annette Island is the 110-mile-long Prince of Wales Island, which gives protection to these waters and beckons one to explore it instead of turning northeast to Ketchikan. And further to the west is the wide-open Pacific, which finally reaches the shores of Russia from which came the early explorers of the region we are now cruising.

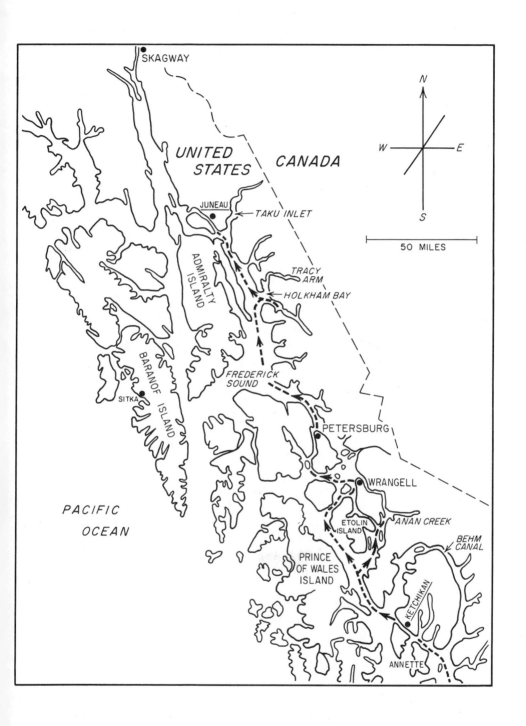

SKAGWAY

UNITED
STATES

CANADA

N

W   E

S

50 MILES

JUNEAU

TAKU INLET

ADMIRALTY
ISLAND

TRACY
ARM

HOLKHAM BAY

BARANOF
ISLAND

FREDERICK
SOUND

SITKA

PETERSBURG

PACIFIC

OCEAN

WRANGELL

ETOLIN
ISLAND

ANAN CREEK

BEHM
CANAL

PRINCE
OF WALES
ISLAND

KETCHIKAN

ANNETTE

CHAPTER 5

Ketchikan to Juneau

After several days of cruising the more primitive waterways of British Columbia and those of southeastern Alaska, the city of Ketchikan appears on the scene almost as a surprise. Settled beneath the brow of a vast icefield and neatly shelved at sea level along the Tongass Narrows, the city bustles with activity. For many years Ketchikan has been the salmon capitol of the world; now its lumber and pulp industries are rapidly becoming runners-up in its economy. These rich but more prosaic industries are counterbalanced by reflections of a unique past, such as the brightly painted totem poles and Indian community houses, which are landmarks in town and in adjoining forest clearings outskirting Ketchikan.

Another contrast we encountered during a recent July cruise was that of watching water skiers skimming across sunflecked waters directly below the perpetual snowfields that cover the city's mountain backdrop. Along the main business thoroughfare, contrasts continue in the shopping area. Alaskan gems, jewelry and costly furs are featured in one store, perhaps alongside a miner's outfitting concern or rifle shop. Adjoining these, another store will specialize in carved ivory, Indian mukluks, extravagantly furred parkas or totem replicas—while interspersed will be the ubiquitous bait-and-tackle supplier.

Many of Ketchikan's totem poles have been moved from more remote regions and brought to a point on Tongass Narrows, just 3 miles south of town. Since the end of the 19th century the art of totem carving has become lost, and the remaining poles will be kept on display for posterity through the efforts of the United States Forest Service. Unfortunately many of these historic Indian treasures were destroyed by well-meaning but uninformed missionaries who thought the totems were heathen idols. There is, in fact, no religious significance attached to these carvings.

Indian ceremonial house, near Ketchikan, Alaska.

Because these Indian tribes had no written language, the totems told a story in hieroglyphs of certain events that occurred in their own or in ancestors' lives; and in part served somewhat as a family crest or coat of arms.

Ketchikan, and Juneau to the north, are centers for southeastern Alaska's network of flying-boat, seaplane and helicopter transportation. Trunk airlines operate from Annette Island's airport, and passengers make the 20-mile flight to Ketchikan's waterfront in amphibians. Scheduled and charter air service link the scores of fishing villages, cannery ports, hunting and fishing areas, in the triangle formed by Ketchikan, Sitka and Juneau, that can only be reached by float planes or helicopters. If time permits, those cruising these waters should make the round-trip flight from Ketchikan to Juneau to see from the air a portion of Alaska that can be viewed by no other means of transportation.

Out of Ketchikan, there are two water routes that may be taken to reach the next major town of Wrangell: either a northwesterly course up Clarence Strait, leaving Etolin Island to starboard, then heading north through Stikine Strait; or the more picturesque route, which we followed by cruising northeasterly through Ernest Sound between Etolin Island and Cleveland Peninsula, along Seward Passage to Anan Creek and proceeding north along the eastern shoreline of Wrangell Island.

One of our main reasons for taking this narrow back-route to Wrangell (other than that "it was there") was an opportunity to see and photograph the Alaskan black bears fishing for salmon below the falls at Anan Creek.

This is an area reserved for hunting with cameras only, and it is said that because these bears have been protected, they have increased in numbers in the Falls area and pay little attention to tourists who come to watch them feeding. We arrived at Humpback Bay, the anchorage into which Anan Creek flows, in the midst of a driving rainstorm, but the moisture did nothing to dampen the enthusiasm of our party for a short overland hike to "the bear place."

Once ashore we found ourselves in a true rain forest. The trail was dark and wet under a dense canopy of trees. It was quiet, with only a faint sound of distant falls and the occasional shriek of a bird alerted by our approach. Suddenly our leader stopped. "A bear track!" There was no mistaking the big pawprint impressed in the mud before us. We paused. "I thought the bears were on the *other* side of the creek." "Black bears won't hurt you, only brown ones are mean," someone said unconvincingly. Finally curiosity overrode our apprehension and we hurried along the trail, which opened at a series of rushing falls. A few yards below us, thousands of salmon were flinging themselves upstream on their headlong rush to spawn. Masses of them hurtled through the air to land in slacker waters, pausing only momentarily before jumping again and again to reach their destination. Then an enormous black bear emerged at streamside, ambled slowly over the rocks to a shallow pool, and then stretched out a huge paw toward a jumping fish. I should have copied the bear's measured

Taking the dinghy ashore at Anan Creek, for a glimpse of salmon-fishing black bears.

movements when I adjusted my camera. Just as the bear success-fully picked a salmon from the water and held it in his mouth—the perfect picture—I hit the wrong button. The shutter would not work. Meanwhile the bear padded off into the woods with his fish, and *my* picture.

Out of Humpback Bay, a northwest heading leads to Blake Channel, through the 100-yard-wide Narrows to Eastern Passage, at which terminus is Point Highfield, the northerly tip of Wrangell Island. The city of Wrangell lies on the westerly side of Point Highfield in a nearly landlocked harbor. This is a port of call for all steamers, and since the late 1800's it has been an outfitting center for those seeking gold, fish, or hunting wild-game trophies near the banks of the Stikine River. One of Alaska's major gold-mining sources, the Stikine winds down from the northeastern mountains for over a hundred miles.

Wrangell is a compact little harbor settlement of about 1600 residents. First settled by the Russians in 1834 as a fur-trading post, its steep-roofed buildings huddle together as if for protec-tion against the magnitude of its bordering mountain terrain. We stopped at their well-built, small-boat harbor and walked the short distance into town for a fresh crab and shrimp lunch, and later inspected some of Wrangell's fine collection of totem poles.

In early afternoon we cast off for the 40-mile run to Petersburg on Mitkof Island, heading westerly between several islets and the two large islands of Zarembo and Mitkof. At Point Alexander to starboard, our course swings north to cruise up famous Wrangell Narrows. Here if ever, a sharp watch is necessary both for drift and for the many buoys marking the winding but well-dredged channel. (The only dredged channel in fact, between Victoria, B.C., and Juneau.) But the watcher cannot complain, either in Wrangell Narrows or in any of the other magnificent waterways. The scenery is so compelling in color and form, in sunshine or rain, that watching is not a duty, but rather a privilege, in cruising this Inside Passage.

All the greens of the spectrum line the Narrows' undulating corridor, turning the watery labyrinth to a matching hue. Now and then we pass a small clearing where a cabin and a few outbuildings bespeak of the trapper or the homesteader hewing his livelihood from this rugged, still-new land.

Before we are even ready to end our day's cruise, we round a bend in the Narrows to find that the vista ahead has suddenly opened to a greater water expanse backed by 4000-foot, snow-capped mountains. We've arrived at Petersburg, bordering Frederick Sound.

Our arrival that evening at Petersburg was well timed. The tide was ebbing and taking out with it a giant iceberg which had, for most of the day, been blocking the small-boat harbor. As we moved into our slip we could see the great berg moving slowly down the Narrows, shimmering rose-gold and blue in the waning sunlight. Nearby, fishing boats were unloading their cargoes of salmon, halibut, cod and crab. And though midday had been warm, as the sun dipped below the western mountains, air temperature sank to 37 degrees.

Petersburg is a base for a number of scenic guided tours, by comfortable charter cruisers, to such points of interest as Leconte and Baird Glaciers only a few miles to the south or north, respectively. It is from these tremendous ice fields that such bergs as we had recently seen are sloughed off, occasionally to drift into Petersburg's snug harbor. Baird Glacier, which heads Thomas Bay, is the most southerly nesting place for the Arctic tern and other sea and shore birds, affording an interesting cruise-tour for the bird watcher. Other tours by land are arranged for those who wish to visit Petersburg's fish-processing plants, to explore the nearby muskeg with its acres of brilliant wild flowers, to inspect an experimental fur farm or to hunt on bountiful Mitkof Island for deer, brown, black and grizzly bears, mountain goats or waterfowl.

At Petersburg and at most of Alaska's major southeastern cities, a new activity is becoming popular with those who wish to hunt, fish or camp in virgin areas inaccessible except by air. Inexpensive charter flights from principal southeastern Alaskan communities will carry a party and their gear to any one of the 142 Wilderness Cabin sites which have been built by the United States Forest Service and native Alaskan sportsmen. These modern A-frame cabins are well stocked with utensils, firewood and cookstoves, and for those at a lake site, a boat is also provided for the visitor's use. Food and a bedroll, and possibly a 3-h.p. outboard, are all the traveler need bring. There is no charge for the use of these cabins or boats, but a five-day occupancy limit is maintained during the seasons in which they are most sought. In other words, one's air fare for flying in and out of his campsite (which may run from $50 to $100 per party, depending on the distance covered) is the only cost for such a five-day vacation.

Much credit is due the Alaska Sportsmen's Council for their efforts and donations toward the development of these Wilderness Cabins. Part of construction costs are derived from the Golden North Salmon Derby, held annually in Juneau; while other contributions of time and money are donated by private enterprise. Those who have sampled luxurious living in the Wilderness Cabins are, needless to say, extravagant in praise of this (ad)venture. As one guest remarked, "At last I've found a mountain cabin where the office can *never* call me, and where the trout *never* get away!"

The distance between Petersburg and Juneau is just over 100 miles, which could well be covered in a day's easy cruise. But even the most fleeting glance at a chart shows a wealth of arms and bays branching off Stephens Passage. Their entrances only hint at the culminating grandeur awaiting those who cruise a little further to explore (particularly) Endicott and Tracy Arms, extending off Holkham Bay. This area, also referred to as Ford's Terror Scenic Area, embraces nearly 14,000 acres of tidewater valleys bordered by abruptly upthrust mountains. The fiords terminate in their eastern extremities with mammoth glaciers,

Icebergs in Holkham Bay, near Endicott Arm, Alaska.

pieces of which break away in midsummer to move about majestically with the changing tides, often out into Stephens Passage and beyond.

Our first cruise into Holkham Bay and Endicott Arm occurred in a late afternoon. There was a high overcast, with skies and water both the exact color of dull steel; but the grayness, which seemed to extend into infinity, only served to intensify the refracted brilliant blues of icebergs floating all about us. This awesome seascape might well have been captioned "The Bitter End of Nowhere," so did its coloring depict a feeling of coldness and isolation. We dropped anchor for the night at a small indention called Sum Dum Bay, which lies a few miles to the southeast of Endicott's entrance. On the following morning, however, we awakened to brilliant sunshine, exposing the wooded and granite walls of Endicott's fiord and its bergs sparkling, this time, under cloudless skies. The scenic metamorphosis was from winter to summer, making the balance of our cruise through Endicott and Tracy Arms another splendid day of sightseeing.

From this midpoint along Stephens Passage, before continuing directly through Gastineau Channel to Juneau, one should take a starboard course at Point Arden and cruise up 16-mile-long Taku Inlet to view the spectacular sight of world-famous Taku

Small-boat Harbor, Juneau, Alaska, where tidal ranges vary up to 20 feet.

Glacier. Alternatively, this particular run might be included in the many day-cruises one may have on his itinerary while using Juneau as a base port.

Here at the State's capital city, the pleasure-boat visitor will find excellent facilities awaiting him at Juneau's small-boat harbors where fuel, supplies and good restaurants are all within walking distance of his slip. Moored in the same harbors are comfortable cruisers for charter for those wishing guided hunting or fishing trips to some of the prime fish and game areas surrounding Juneau. Land tours by taxi or sightseeing buses may be arranged with Travel Services in town as well as airplane or helicopter scenic flights, which are becoming increasingly popular.

Although Juneau is not Alaska's oldest city, it was the very first Territorial white settlement founded under the American flag. Other principal southeastern Alaska communities had diverse early settlers. Sitka and Wrangell were originally Russian inhabited, Petersburg had Scandinavian ancestry, and other cities were first settled by the Finnish—all, of course, preceded by Indians. Not yet 100 years old, Juneau first became a gold-mining camp in 1880, a year after gold was first discovered by Joe Juneau and Richard Harris. Three years later it had risen to the status of Alaska's gold center, and flourished as such for many years. In 1917, the mines on Douglas Island across from Juneau were flooded, and in 1944 the last of Juneau's big mines were depleted, thus ending a colorful era so well marked in history.

The transition from the lusty gold-seeking days, however, has been toward an increasingly stable economy which is due in no small measure to the vast network of waterways and airways radiating from Juneau. Commercial fishing and forestry are today's major industries of the area, with tourism a rising challenge.

One of the most popular side trips for newcomers to Juneau is the 13-mile drive from town to Mendenhall Glacier. This slowly receding glacial moraine still contains remnants of the great forest it sheared off in its long-ago descent to Auke Lake Valley. Footpaths have been carved along the side boundaries of this nearly 2 mile-wide glacier, to permit the hiker to look

Dawes Glacier, Alaska. A few boats make it this far, nosing between icebergs.

down into some of its massive crevasses. From a flight over Juneau, Mendenhall is but one of a dozen glaciers that can be seen in this immediate vicinity.

Going from cloud tops to underground, visitors may wish to tour the historic Alaska Juneau Gold Mine, where a train ride through a mile-long tunnel takes one out to the face of Mt. Roberts, high above the city. From this point, a reconditioned road and bridge lead to some of the old mine buildings; ore samples are on display there, along with tools and conveyors used during the days when millions of dollars of gold ore was taken from the A.J. Mine and sent to Juneau's mill for refining.

Early in August, the annual Golden North Salmon Derby attracts thousands of residents and visitors to vie for heaviest salmon brought to dock. Over $17,000 in prizes are given each year to winners in this popular fishing contest. Revenue from the sale of fish caught is donated to a host of worthy enterprises, ranging from scholarships to materials for Wilderness Cabins.

For those bringing their own boats up from the south to Juneau for a period of sightseeing and exploring, there remain innumerable return routes other than those taken cruising north, and each of these presents new vistas of never-ending interest. As for us, book pages are running out. Regretfully, we must make Juneau the end of our cruise.

Appendix to Part III

Books and Charts
Facilities and Supplies
Electric/Electronic Equipment
Types of Boats Suitable
Chartering
Clothing
Customs Clearance in and Out of Canada and U.S.
Imports
Steamer, Ferry and Air Transportation
Table of Distances

BOOKS & CHARTS

Tide and current tables published by the United States and Canadian Governments, in addition to the charts available from the U. S. Coast & Geodetic Survey, U. S. Hydrographic Office and Canadian Hydrographic Office, are essential to safe and enjoyable cruising in these waters. The tide and current tables will serve to determine times of departure from one harbor to the next, to take advantage of favorable currents and to avoid areas where maximum floods or ebbs can create turbulent and sometimes dangerous water. Publications and charts are available at all the principal ports, such as Victoria, Vancouver, Nanaimo, and Prince Rupert, British Columbia; and Ketchikan, Wrangell, Petersburg and Juneau, Alaska. It requires more than 50 charts to cover the route from Victoria, B.C. to Juneau, Alaska, so detailed are many of them.

The most valuable aid to navigation besides the government publications is the *Marine Atlas, Vol. II*, edited by Frank Morris, W. R. Heath and Amos Burg, published by P.B.I. Co., P.O.

Box 54, Seattle, Washington. It covers all the west coast of Vancouver Island, the inside-Inside Passage routes from the Island to Prince Rupert, B.C., and both the mainland and Islands in Alaska to Skagway, above Juneau. Their *Marine Atlas Vol. I* details the waters between Olympia and Port Hardy on Vancouver Island. Courses, distances and detailed information on facilities are shown in chart form, augmented with air photos.

Guide To Alaska by Lou Jacobin. (Guide to Alaska Co., Juneau, Alaska, or 6015 Santa Monca Blvd., Los Angeles, Calif.)

Alaska Sportsman monthly magazine (Northeast Publishing Co., Box 1271, Juneau, Alaska).

Northwest Passages by Bruce Calhoun (Miller Freeman Publications, Inc., 500 Howard St., San Francisco, Calif.)

FACILITIES & SUPPLIES—BRITISH COLUMBIA AND ALASKA

There is no scarcity of fuel and supplies along the more direct routes between Victoria, B.C. and the northwest end of Vancouver Island; even along the inside-Inside Passages it is seldom more than fifty miles between supplies. Some of the longer inlets may require 100 miles of cruising, considering the distance up and back to a lumbering operation or fisherman's supply depot. Once past Cape Caution, to the northeast of the extremity of Vancouver Island, the distances between fuel and supply depots become greater. The longest distances between them are roughly 100 miles, as one is heading northwest toward Juneau, Alaska.

Unique to this area is the completeness of supply stores that are usually adjacent to fueling docks—with apparel, fishing gear, food and common engine-repair parts. These are stocked for the operation and provisioning of commercial tugs and fishing boats. In some of the most remote areas there will be a marine railway or "grid" for boats of up to 30 or 40 feet in length. The grid is simply a heavily built platform on pilings, 5 to 7 feet below high water level, with a bulkhead along the shore side. A boat in need of bottom repairs ties to the vertical bulkhead, or in some cases to a group of piles, and waits for the tide to go out. With the range of tide between low and high water as much as 25 feet in the more northern reaches of this area, a good many hours of repair work can be performed before the next rising tide floats the boat off the grid. In some of the larger harbors, grids are available for boats of up to 100 feet in length.

Radio Communication to shore-based public telephone operators is not as reliable as along the coasts of California, Oregon and Washington, because terrain and canyon-like channels limit the range of the average marine radiotelephone. The British Columbia Telephone Co. has stations at Vancouver and Prince Rupert, and the Alaska Communication System—operated by the U. S. Air Force—has stations at Ketchikan and Juneau. Weather reports are broadcast by both groups. In addition, many British Columbia communities are equipped with radio links using VHF equipment and repeater stations high atop the hills and mountains, and will handle radio traffic to mainland cities.

ELECTRIC/ELECTRONIC EQUIPMENT

In British Columbia and Alaska the ground tackle needed is little different from that required for anchoring along the California, Oregon and Washington coasts. The depths of the coves, inlets and harbors, however, dictate the need for more than average lengths of chain and anchor rode, and an electric-power anchor windlass.

When tying alongside log booms and log-supported floats, pneumatic fenders should be used. In addition, it is helpful to lash a lead ball, of the type used on seine nets, to the lower end of each fender, to keep them in a vertical position between the hull and the log. Without the sinker weight, the fenders will float horizontally and be of little value.

Radio navigation aids are few and far between, and basically of no great need because of the canyon channels. Depth sounders, on the other hand, are of great assistance in anchoring, due to the steep slopes of beaches and the depths that are common even close to shore.

Other electronic equipment helpful in cruising these waters includes automatic pilot, radiotelephone and radar. The latter is particularly helpful if one plans to run at night, even though no fog is present, because the topography of the area gives sharp definition to the inlets and channels and shows them on the radar-scope as precisely as they are seen on charts.

TYPES OF BOATS SUITABLE

Nearly all types of power boats are suitable for cruising British Columbia and Alaska waters along the passages discussed in the last five chapters. Fast day-cruisers are used extensively because their speed shortens the time for runs between fuel and supply de-pots and attractive campsites or hotel accommodations. Larger and heavier power boats seldom encounter water passages too shallow for their hulls, and again, the wealth of overnight facili-ties precludes even the slowest of such craft having to seek an-chorages after darkness. Each year finds a larger number of people trailing their boats from distant ports to launch them in north-west waters for extended summer vacations in these scenic water-ways. Although sailboats are encountered occasionally in the more windy passages, the Canadian San Juan Island region is not con-ducive to good sailing, simply because it is protected by moun-tains and other land windbreaks. Moreover, strong tidal currents often necessitate greater hull speed than the average sailboat's auxiliary can manage.

CHARTER BOATS

As we have brought out in the Introduction to this book, there is no Pacific Coast boat chartering on a large commercial scale, as is done from south-Atlantic ports. A few private boat charters are available from such British Columbian harbors as Vancouver and Victoria, and in Ketchikan and Juneau, Alaska. Advertisements of these operators and details of their services can be found in such magazines as *Alaska Sportsman*, and *SEA and Pacific Motor Boat*, and certain other outdoor or hunting/fishing periodicals. An alter-nate source of charter information would be through yacht brokers in Seattle, Washington, and Vancouver, B.C.

CLOTHING

Summer temperatures in British Columbia and southeastern Alaska will vary from the high 70's to occasional lows of around 40 degrees. There have been occasions when no rain has fallen for a three-week span, but this is not to be depended upon. Several warm sweaters, wool slacks and a water-repellent jacket should be included in clothing brought for this climate, as well as shorts or summer dresses for sunny afternoons. A basic wardrobe of informal, sports-type clothes is the rule—the only areas where dinner clothes are generally worn for evening are in Victoria and Vancouver at their larger hotels or restaurants. For those planning special hunting, fishing or hiking expeditions, the individual pursuit will indicate suitable apparel, based on what might be taken for other outdoor areas having comparable temperature variations.

CUSTOMS CLEARANCE IN AND OUT OF CANADA AND UNITED STATES

Entry ports into British Columbia (of concern to those cruising the Inside Passage) include Vancouver, West Vancouver YC, Victoria, Nanaimo, Sidney, Powell River, Bedwell Harbor, Boundary Bay (Point Roberts), Campbell River, Namu and Prince Rupert. There are also Bamfield and Port Alberni on the outside of Vancouver Island. Except for Saturdays, Sundays and holidays or after regular business hours, there is no charge for entry into Canada. No passports are required for U.S. citizens going into Canada, but it is well to have one's proof of citizenship available. Firearms and animals require special handling.

For those returning from Canada, the U.S. entry ports nearest Canadian waters are Bellingham, Blaine, Port Angeles, Port Townsend, Anacortes, Friday Harbor, Roche Harbor, Everett and Seattle. During business hours on weekdays there are no Customs charges; however, both Friday and Roche Harbors may be used for Customs clearance back into the United States on weekends and holidays, between June first and Labor Day, for a nominal fee (approximately $3.00) through the courtesies of The Washington Interclub Association and yacht clubs in the Puget Sound area.

IMPORTS

There is no duty on merchandise up to $100 brought from Canada into the United States. There is no limitation on cigarettes for personal use, but not more than 100 cigars may be included. Not over one quart of alcoholic beverages per person may be brought from Canada into the United States or taken from the U.S. into Canada.

STEAMER, FERRY AND AIR TRANSPORTATION

From Seattle, Washington:
Western Air Lines, with stops at Ketchikan and Juneau, daily.

Alaska Airlines, daily flights to Juneau.

From Vancouver, B.C.:
Alaska Cruise Lines, Ltd., with stops at Ketchikan, Juneau, Skagway and Haines (May through September schedules, every four days).

Canadian National Steamship, with stops at Prince Rupert, Ketchikan, Wrangell, Juneau and Skagway (May through August schedules, every eight days).

Canadian Pacific Steamship Co., with stops at Prince Rupert, Ketchikan, Wrangell, Juneau and Skagway (June, July and August schedules, every eight days).

Canadian Pacific Airlines to Prince Rupert, daily schedules.

From Vancouver Island:
British Columbia Ferries between Kelsey Bay and Prince Rupert, B.C.

From Prince Rupert, B. C.:
Alaska State Ferry System, with stops at Ketchikan, Wrangell, Petersburg, Sitka, Juneau, Skagway and Haines (during summer, departures are approximately daily).

From Ketchikan and Juneau, Alaska:
Alaska Coastal-Ellis Airlines; scheduled and charter flights throughout all of southeastern Alaska.

APPROXIMATE DISTANCES IN NAUTICAL MILES
BETWEEN BRITISH COLUMBIA AND ALASKAN PORTS

	Miles
Victoria, B.C. to Nanaimo, B.C.	64
Victoria, B.C. to Vancouver, B.C.	72
Victoria to Campbell River	142
Victoria to Cape Caution	270
Vancouver, B.C. to Powell River	68
Vancouver, B.C. to Campbell River	99
Vancouver, B.C. to Yaculta Rapids	110
Vancouver, B.C. to Cape Caution (via Yaculta)	237
Cape Caution to Bella Bella	68
Bella Bella to Butedale	80
Butedale to Prince Rupert	100
Prince Rupert to Ketchikan, Alaska	85
Ketchikan, Alaska to Wrangell (via Anan Creek)	98
Ketchikan, Alaska to Wrangell (via Stikine St.)	88
Wrangell to Petersburg via Wrangell Narrows	40
Petersburg to Holkham Bay (& Sum Dum Cove)	74
Holkham Bay to Juneau	46
Victoria to Juneau	954

INDEX